# REVIEWS OF NATIONAL POLICIES FOR EDUCATION

# ITALY

ORGANISATION FOR ECONOMIC CO-OPERATION AND DEVELOPMENT

# ORGANISATION FOR ECONOMIC CO-OPERATION AND DEVELOPMENT

Pursuant to Article 1 of the Convention signed in Paris on 14th December 1960, and which came into force on 30th September 1961, the Organisation for Economic Co-operation and Development (OECD) shall promote policies designed:

- to achieve the highest sustainable economic growth and employment and a rising standard of living in Member countries, while maintaining financial stability, and thus to contribute to the development of the world economy;
- to contribute to sound economic expansion in Member as well as non-member countries in the process of economic development; and
- to contribute to the expansion of world trade on a multilateral, non-discriminatory basis in accordance with international obligations.

The original Member countries of the OECD are Austria, Belgium, Canada, Denmark, France, Germany, Greece, Iceland, Ireland, Italy, Luxembourg, the Netherlands, Norway, Portugal, Spain, Sweden, Switzerland, Turkey, the United Kingdom and the United States. The following countries became Members subsequently through accession at the dates indicated hereafter: Japan (28th April 1964), Finland (28th January 1969), Australia (7th June 1971), New Zealand (29th May 1973), Mexico (18th May 1994), the Czech Republic (21st December 1995), Hungary (7th May 1996), Poland (22nd November 1996) and Korea (12th December 1996). The Commission of the European Communities takes part in the work of the OECD (Article 13 of the OECD Convention).

Publié en français sous le titre :
EXAMENS DES POLITIQUES NATIONALES D'ÉDUCATION
ITALIE

# FOREWORD

This volume presents the Educational Policy Review of Italy undertaken in early 1998 at the request of the Italian authorities. A background report prepared by the Italian Ministry of Education (*Ministero della Pubblica Istruzione*) for the examiners has been published separately as *Rapporto di Base sulla Politica Scolastica Italiana*.

The Examiners' Report contained in this volume was presented by Mr. Norberto Bottani, Director of the Unit for Educational Research (Department of Education, Canton of Geneva) and Mr. T.J. Alexander, Director of DEELSA (Directorate for Education, Employment, Labour and Social Affairs of OECD) at the Forum P.A. (*Pubblica Amministrazione*) on 7 May 1998 in Rome in the presence of the Italian Minister for Education, Mr. Luigi Berlinguer.

The examiners for the review were Norberto Bottani (Switzerland), Martin Carnoy (USA), Gregor Ramsey, rapporteur (Australia) and Alejandro Tiana Ferrer (Spain). The report is published on the responsibility of the Secretary-General of the OECD.

# TABLE OF CONTENTS

# THE CONTEXT

Over the past decade, change in education has been a salient feature in most countries. The increasing number of young people staying on at school, the influence of the changing nature of work on educational expectations, growing youth unemployment in many countries, and the impact of technological change are all influencing the debate on education. These influences have impacted on national policies, including educational structure and organisation, the nature, development and teaching of curriculum, and the role and responsibilities of schools, causing significant change in traditional educational frameworks.

All of these trends manifest themselves differently from country to country. This is certainly true in Italy where educational change has been slow to take hold, but which now commands close government attention. Italy has seen significant economic development over past decades. It is a key player in the European Union and, as a member of the Group of Seven, it is also a major player in the world economy. Its products are available on the global market place; its technical achievements, the success of the small business sector and the high standard of its design make it a country which others see as having important skills well worth emulating. Despite these successes, there is concern that Italy's educational growth and development has not matched its outstanding economic development and has not perhaps served the country's new needs as well as it might.

Italy, too, has a long heritage which has impacted the world for more than 2 000 years. This heritage is passed on to citizens in a traditional way through the education system, setting up a natural tension between the transmission of the country's long established culture and the requirements of the new economic age. Social traditions also have their impact. Italy is a country coming to unification from a long history of state or city independence. These differences of identity coming from historical independence make the country more complex than a simplistic distinction between the North and South. Yet it is this richness from a spirit of individualism and entrepreneurship coupled with the country's diversity which gives it strength and flexibility. Italy has wide cultural diversity which is still bound by common language and common values. Although often apparently politically untidy, this variety provides a cultural dynamism which seems so often to be lacking in countries that are more monocultural.

Italy has had centralised education system since the 19th century. It has been important in sustaining the country's traditions and has provided the cement for combining diversity into a manageable whole. Centralised curriculum has made it possible for the best of the culture, the best of science and mathematics, the best of technical skills and knowledge to be made available to young people across the country. Yet such a centralised approach does not allow sufficiently for responsibility for what children learn to rest where it should, at the school level. Nor does it allow regions or provinces to take into account local requirements and local traditions which in many eyes are as important a part of the school curriculum as is the national core curriculum. The country is now endeavouring to reconcile the need for a national framework which will guarantee meeting local needs and aspirations and ensure that Italy's natural diversity will be fully reflected in its education.

These are some of the issues that often remain in the background when any reform of education is being contemplated. Italy's position when compared with OECD averages or those of the G7 countries show that there has been significant development, but there is some way to go if it is to lead on some indicators, and be closer to averages on others.

Because the trends outlined above have led to considerable political attention being given to education in recent times, it is important to set the political context. Change in a democratic society must come through the working out of the country's political processes. This is as true in Italy as it is in any other. In this section we outline the review team's perspective on the political context and processes that are in operation.

## THE POLITICAL CONTEXT

Political instability has long been one of the salient features of Italian democracy. Since the first Parliament was opened in 1948, Italy has had 45 different governments and 30 different Education Ministers. Only two remained in office throughout the lifetime of a parliament, from 1963 to 1968 and from 1983 to 1987, and there were eight between 1953 and 1958 and five between 1979 and 1983. The present government came to power in May 1996. The political landscape has been changed by the emergence of two broad coalitions. In principle that should provide greater stability. The government has the time to undertake and carry through far-reaching reforms.

There is nothing new about the difficulties facing the government, whether public debt, management of the social welfare system, pensions and the burden they represent on the public purse, or unemployment and development in the south of the country. But the changed context, with the break-up of the party system and action to tackle corruption, is leading the government, which for the first time since 1948 is based on a broad left majority, to raise standards in public life and

strive to realise a number of core ideas. European convergence has figured promi-
nently. Italy was one of the initiators of the Treaty of Rome and is in the first wave
of countries to adopt the single European currency. Another central idea is the
reform of government and public administration. Against this background, the government has made education a top priority and has embarked on a fundamental
reform of the entire education system.

The reform was long awaited. There had been no thorough overhaul of the education system since the 1920s, causing an extraordinary accumulation of unresolved
issues and problems. There has been no shortage of reform projects or education
bills, but none had gained enough support across the political spectrum to become
law. In the post-war period alone the Gonella project (1951) was succeeded by Aldo
Moro's ten-year plan (1958) which subsequently became a three-year financial plan
(1962-65), followed by Luigi Gui's guidelines (1964), the new schools plan (1971-75),
the Biasini Commission's plan (1971) and, more recently, the Brocca Commission
report (1988). The talk in educational circles was of the "impossible reform", and it
became the subject of many articles in newspapers, magazines and specialist jour-
nals. Unable to embark on any fundamental transformation, successive governments
merely tinkered with the system. Through experimental schemes and "assisted
projects", fairly substantial changes were occasionally made to the orientation of
certain streams and subjects, but not to the overall pattern of its administration.

Thorough reform of the education system is a hazardous undertaking in any
country, and one which few governments wish to embark on, as the venerable age
of most educational institutions in OECD Member states shows. In Italy, however,
reform seems to be even more difficult than elsewhere. One of the reasons is perhaps that since unification, political life has been determined by the constant quest
for balance between Rome, the regions, the provinces and even the cities, which
have a long tradition of independence. As education is one of the most potent sym-
bols of the state, it is hardly surprising that the foundations of the system were laid
during periods when the desire for unity was particularly strong. Thus, the Casati
law was drafted in 1859, shortly after unification, the Gentile law in 1923 after the
First World War, and the Codignola law after the Second World War and adoption of
the new constitution. Even so, however, the first two laws, adopted in periods of
authoritarian government, were in fact never passed by Parliament, while the third
law was only passed fifteen years after it was first tabled (Visalberghi, 1981).

Under these circumstances, it is hardly surprising that the government's reform
proposals should have aroused so much interest, enthusiasm and hope. They
tackle the difficult and burdensome legacy of a system which discourages initiative,
checks enthusiasm and stifles ambition. A great deal of courage is certainly necessary to set about reform on this scale, but this long-awaited initiative has widespread support both in public opinion and in educational circles. It is clearly the

government's intention to review not only the nature and organisation of the education system but also the way it is administered and the wider relationships between education, the economy and society. The reform does not stand in isolation. The measure to make schools autonomous is part of a much broader movement to decentralise and reform the state, involving a reform of the constitution that is currently being debated in a joint parliamentary commission whose members are drawn from both chambers. Furthermore, the reform proposals do not only concern state, or public, schools; they also extend to training courses that do not fall within the purview of the Education Ministry, and even to private education. The key word is integration. The reform reflects the quest for a comprehensive vision of the role of education in society; it seeks to build a coherent, decentralised and effective education system.

Italian politics are currently in upheaval. Educational reforms are only part of a picture which also includes reforms drawn up by the Labour and Social Security Ministries concerning employment, training, apprenticeships and employment-training contracts and, on the broader canvas, decentralisation and the reform of the state. And these are only the sectors which concern our review directly. Other aspects include agreements with social partners and agreements between ministries and regions, or between the regions themselves. Some legislation is still under review or in the consultative phase; some bills have been adopted by the government and are now being discussed in parliamentary committees; and some have reached the end of their journey and have been passed by Parliament, creating an enormous amount of work in order to draw up the corresponding implementing decrees. The legislative landscape changes week by week. The contrast that used to exist in Italy between the dynamism of industry and society on the one hand and the inertia of government and the inefficiency of Parliament on the other is now a thing of the past.

## THE REFORM AND ITS IMPLEMENTATION

The scale of the reform is considerable. It concerns the nature and aims of education, changes to educational cycles, an extension of compulsory schooling, changes in the *maturità* (the examination at the end of the secondary education cycle), the promotion of vocational and technical education, the creation of a national system for evaluation as a counterpart to autonomy, and an overhaul of the way the whole system is administered.

Implementing reform on such a scale creates its own difficulties. In the 1960s, Italy, like many other countries, sought to reform the entire educational system, but plans were thwarted by an inability to achieve political consensus on a comprehensive project. Gradual and isolated reforms were introduced, but the method was not particularly effective. Changes were mainly brought about through experimental schemes, which often produced interesting results. Some of these schemes were evaluated and found suitable to be extended to the system as a whole, and were in fact sanctioned by Parliament in the shape of educational reforms, for elementary schools and the technical and vocational institutes for example. In order to break the deadlock, the present government has opted for a piecemeal approach, for two reasons. First, the planned reform is on such a vast scale that a range of legislative, regulatory and contractual options are needed to cover all the various components. Second, it seems more realistic to seek agreement and consensus on elements of a plan rather than on a comprehensive package of reforms, which would easily provoke opposition on political or ideological grounds. This of course raises the question of whether, on completion of the process, the diverse elements will combine to produce a coherent whole.

In the introduction to the education reform bill, the government states that it deliberately chose not to place a draft before Parliament straight away; it had first wanted to hold a nation-wide consultation on the general directions of the planned reform. It did so because it considered that education matters are not the preserve of any political majority; they concern all the groups making up the national community. The government's responsibility here is not to impose its own ideas, but to interpret the concerns of society and make proposals to Parliament that will provide effective responses, while respecting the standpoints of the various political parties. The consultation proved most successful; it had the merit of opening up a broad debate about education issues and to draw the attention of public opinion to the problems that arise in education, which had not been the case in Italy for a considerable time. The minister received over a thousand replies between January and June. As a result, when framing the education reform bill, the public's response was taken into account as fully as possible.

One of the effects of embarking on a reform that affects all aspects of teaching and education is to create and maintain the impetus. This was clearly the minister's intention, and it appears to have been entirely successful. Of course we encountered scepticism during our visits, often from people who were thoroughly ill-informed about the nature and aims of the reforms, a point to which we shall return. We also heard many criticisms, some of them quite fierce, which were well-argued and worthy of consideration. But we generally found that these criticisms were directed at the thrust of a reform, at the way a given proposal had been shaped or its possible consequences, rather than at the principle of reform itself. There thus appears to be a general consensus both on the need to bring the system up to date and on the principle of reform. We are convinced that the impetus that already exists will lead to substantial progress.

Not all the criticisms, of course, are as worthy of respect as those formulated by experts, researchers or politicians which we mentioned above and regard as positive contributions to the debate. We refer here to the way in which discussions have been taken into the political arena and arguments and proposals distorted, especially in the media, though Italy clearly does not have a monopoly on such tendencies. However that may be, turning educational reform into a political football could wreck projects which are fundamentally worthwhile. It is perhaps the weakness of such a far-reaching reform that the debate will be a lengthy one and that criticism may take over from objective argument. There is a real risk that the initial support will be lost.

At the same time, other reforms are also under way. They have their own impetus and may move at a faster or slower pace than educational reforms. The instigators of educational reforms could find themselves outstripped as a result of dynamism or activism in certain circles, and this could lead to a significant distortion of initial plans. We are thinking of the current developments in regional vocational training, based on laws that have already been passed. We are also thinking of the discussions on the reform of the state now taking place in both chambers of Parliament. Their results could lead to conclusions that differ from the assumptions on which the autonomy of schools and the overall conduct of education policy have been predicated. We are thinking too, of parliamentary decisions to do with decentralisation, which could lead in directions which do not necessarily tally with the very widely approved objectives of education policy. We see in these factors a risk of distortion, or dilution, which, as a potential threat to the broad consensus on the thrust of the reform, to the ideal of coherence, needs to be taken into consideration and defused.

Lastly, we felt that the wind of reform has blown up a storm in the minds of those involved with education and training, in central government, in the regions, and in political circles in general, who think only in terms of legislation, decrees, framework agreements and so on and may well lose touch with the grassroots reality. It has to be underlined that a reform of this nature calls for long-term vision and a clear perception of the paths to follow.

## SOME OF THE GUIDING PRINCIPLES OF THE REFORM

Faced with this tangle of laws, decrees, agreements, draft framework legislation and so on, we, like many others, sought a guiding principle, a key which would make it possible to situate each disparate element within a coherent whole. We identified some of these ideas. One, for instance, is the idea discussed by the *Commissione dei Saggi*, which touches on the type of education to be given to new and future generations (Commissione dei Saggi, 1997). We shall briefly consider the subject in Chapter 3.

A prime motive often cited for reform is Italy's "education gap". The average education level of the Italian population is one of the lowest in Europe (OECD, 1997, Table A2.1). This is partly due to the historical development of education in Italy, which was long the privilege of the elite. The rest of the population was neglected. Already in the 19th century, Italy was known as the country with the largest number of universities but the lowest level of education (Barbagli, 1974). The expansion of education came late in Italy and the idea of an "education gap" in relation to the other countries of Europe was both widely held and deeply felt. A legendary programme from the early days of television in the 1950s was called "It's never too late", meaning by implication never too late to learn to read and write, and hence to deepen one's culture, to broaden one's mind.[1]

Decentralisation is another guiding principle. The Italian education system has been unarguably too rigid and too highly centralised, with the central administration too cumbersome and unable either to control the working of such a vast system or to take local needs into consideration. It is hardly surprising that many of the people we spoke to regarded the autonomy of schools as the central plank of the whole reform programme. This change raises high hopes, and much concern as well. Autonomy is not an end in itself. It is justified insofar as it helps to improve the quality of education, to motivate teachers and to forge links between schools and their communities. However, the law on autonomy (Law 59/1997, called Bassanini Law), which provides for decentralisation of the entire school system, not simply some parts of it, refers to the role of central government and the autonomy of schools without defining the role of the provinces and regions. Many doubts remain, at least among teachers, as to the relationships or differences between autonomy and decentralisation. Other questions arise as to the likely consequences of this change. Some schools, local authorities and regions will be able to mobilise more resources than others and disparities could well increase considerably. We shall consider the subject in Chapter 5, when we discuss autonomy, assessment and the role of the government in the conduct of education policy.

## THE OECD'S ASSIGNMENT

The Italian authorities asked the OECD to give an "opinion", within a very short space of time, on the proposals for educational reform. The task is a difficult one, because it involves discussing ideas and proposals rather than giving a diagnosis of a situation or an assessment of trends. This difficulty is compounded by the fact that the same ideas and proposals can be put into practice in very different ways. The task is doubly difficult because, rather than taking a mere snapshot of the current situation, it means looking at things both from a historical perspective and with a view to the long term, trying to determine how trends might develop, and trying to anticipate the future. Fortunately, the OECD has long been monitoring education policy in Italy, and in particular conducted two reviews (OECD, 1969 and 1985).

In fact, the assignment turned out to be even harder than we had imagined. The effervescence of Italian politics and a legislative situation that changes week by week expose foreign experts to the risk of losing their bearings in the whirlwind of reform.

But we made a choice, deciding to maintain a certain distance from the froth of day-to-day politics. In the first place, we had a deadline for completion, and were aware that by the time the report was published some comments or proposals would be things of the past. Second, we opted to look at things from a different standpoint, not only because that is part of the way we work but also because we believe it is the standpoint most often forgotten. The standpoint we chose was that of young people, parents and workers who, though they may be informed about the broad thrust of the reform, know nothing of the ideas behind it, the hidden stakes, the agreements and the compromises, and who, to put it bluntly, take no interest in them. What does interest them, by contrast, are simple, clear, transparent ideas. It is with this concern for transparency and clarity that we shall review the proposed reforms.

Lastly, we wish to emphasise that in carrying out our assignment we shall be as balanced as possible. As we said earlier, we read comments and criticisms from all sources. For the first time in the long history of OECD reviews, we even organised two "private" seminars in Rome (private inasmuch as they were not part of the official programme of our visit) to which we invited not only experts known to be in favour of, or even behind, the government's proposals but also experts who had expressed critical or even hostile opinions. We were told that our request had caused a certain stir in the ministry. The minister had understood the reasons for our initiative and accepted them. At the same time, we are aware that there are few unquestionable truths in the field of education. We shall give particular consideration to the possibilities of implementation and to the practical consequences of the various proposals. Rather than indicating a solution, we shall put forward recommendations and, wherever possible, propose a range of options and directions.

Chapter 2 of this report contains a brief review of the state of education in Italy and the relationships between education and the evolving social and employment situation. The following three chapters deal with the reform of education in schools (Chapter 3), transition to working life (Chapter 4), and autonomy, assessment and decentralisation (Chapter 5). Chapter 6 contains our conclusions and recommendations. As is customary, readers are advised not to read that chapter in isolation without first assimilating our comments in the preceding chapters, which are of a different nature and style.

# 2

# ASPECTS OF EDUCATION IN ITALY

It is not our intention here to give a detailed analysis of the state of education in Italy. Others have already done so. However, we did not feel it possible to give an opinion on the proposed reforms untrammelled by any consideration of whether they were legitimate, necessary or appropriate without a short chapter to summarise a few essential facts and describe how we perceive the qualities and possible short-comings of an education system. In doing so, we shall seek to take the traditional OECD approach of setting education in its broad economic and social context.

This would suffice to show the necessity of giving a historical dimension to our approach, since social aspirations and economic development needs are in constant flux. But there are other reasons as well. The first is that schools and particular courses and diplomas have a strong social role. In certain circumstances and at certain times this social image strengthens or deteriorates, and the reasons need to be elucidated. Diplomas and courses serve to crystallise hopes and ambitions, whether of a per-sonal, family or collective nature. They are also the basis on which many firms devise their recruitment programmes or organisational structures. Another reason is that the impact of the reform of an education system cannot be instantaneous, set in place as soon as Parliament votes the laws. The results of even extremely well-prepared reform can take years or even decades to produce the desired results. Rather than taking a snapshot and analysing it, we need to see where a given trend might lead, what a given reform might lead to, in ten or fifteen years' time.

## THE BUILDING OF THE EDUCATION SYSTEM

Italy has a well-established history of teaching institutions, such as its centu-ries-old universities. But in tracing the development of the Italian education sys-tem, we should perhaps start with the Casati law of 1859. Initially limited to Piedmont and Lombardy, it was gradually extended to the entire country as the uni-fication process advanced. The second major stage was the Gentile law of 1923. The system set in place provided primary schools to teach all children, secondary schools preparing for university education and reserved for a limited number, and a range of supplementary courses, general or occupational, which were for those unable to enter secondary schools and did not as a rule lead on to higher education. A few special aspects of the system are worth mentioning.

The first is the slow pace at which enrolment advanced in basic education. The rise in elementary enrolment rates has been sluggish and, at this level, schooling did not become generalised until after the Second World War. As a result, Italy long continued to have a high proportion of illiterates. Concern was voiced back at the start of the century at illiteracy rates among young men conscripted for military service: around one in three in Italy in 1901, under 5 per cent in France, under 1 per cent in Germany (Corridore, 1974). During the first OECD review of Italy (OECD, 1969) the government's background report still laid emphasis on the extent of illiteracy and, more broadly, the low levels of education among the adult population. The proportion of illiterates was as much as 13 per cent in 1951, and 8 per cent in 1961. The average level of education (among the population over 11 years of age) was 2.2 years' schooling in 1901, and just 5 years in 1961. The proportion of people who have not gone beyond elementary school is still as much as 18 per cent in the labour force, and over 50 per cent among the non-active. Italy has experienced greater difficulties than other countries in enrolling all young people in elementary education.

Enrolment in "middle" school, the first cycle of secondary education, took even longer to expand. It only began to take off after the Second World War: enrolment rates rose from 31 per cent in 1951 to 62 per cent in 1961, with marked inequalities between North and South and between boys and girls. Against this background it is easy to see the impact of the Codignola reforms of 1962, establishing a single middle school (abolishing the parallel "paths towards work" – l'avviamento al lavoro) and aiming to provide schooling for all children up to the age of 14. That aim has been accomplished today, but we shall see that the current system, despite rapid expansion of second-cycle enrolment, still bears the imprint of its historical development, leaving a proportion of young people without any vocational qualification after their compulsory schooling.

Another notable aspect of the system's development is the importance attached, even in the Casati law and confirmed by the Gentile measures, to technical education. In Italy this reflected the expectations of the world of work, in particular the workers' co-operatives, which viewed technical education as valuable training for children of modest origins, offering them a skilled job, in contrast to general education. But it is also of interest to emphasise here the value which education policy-makers attached to this type of education: one stream, the physics and mathematics section,[2] allowed access to university. Alongside the ginnasio and the liceo, there was a technical institute and college track, often attracting more students than the lyceums.

Similar innovations were being made at around the same time in a number of European countries. There may have been a variety of reasoning behind them: political – fostering the development of a new middle class; social – offering job and career prospects to young people from modest origins; or economic – underpinning the upsurge of industrialisation and small business creation. The initiative may have come from political circles, industry or indeed the religious orders. Yet the idea found its most striking expression in Italy, where technical education assumed a highly significant place in the overall system.

At the same time the technical institutes, like the lyceums, continued to be reserved for relatively limited numbers. As well as technicians, middle managers and small business owners, there was a need for skilled personnel on the operations side. Training these people was the responsibility of the first-cycle technical schools, and later of the *l'avviamento al lavoro*, but this approach does not appear to have generated a great deal of interest until quite recently, compared to other countries where the focus was in fact on basic vocational training. The reason may also lie in the nature of the skills required. However, vocational institutes[3] were established in 1938, with a three-year cycle (as against five years in the technical institutes and lyceums). For obvious reasons, this change did not come into effect until after the war. They then expanded quite quickly, though without matching the development of the technical institutes, as Table 1 shows.

Table 1. **Breakdown of entrants to the second cycle of secondary education (%)**

|                         | 1951 | 1961 | 1965 |
|-------------------------|------|------|------|
| Lyceums                 | 31.8 | 21.6 | 20.8 |
| Teacher training        | 20.2 | 13.4 | 17.6 |
| Technical institutes    | 28.0 | 39.1 | 41.2 |
| *of which*: industry    | 5.7  | 16.3 | 17.3 |
| Vocational institutes   | 18.3 | 23.3 | 17.2 |
| Others                  | 1.7  | 2.6  | 3.2  |

1. Between 1951 and 1965, total inflows more than trebled.
*Source*: OECD (1969).

As in many other countries, the Labour Ministry held responsibility, in conjunction with the social partners, for vocational training for workers. As from 1951, it introduced courses for young people looking for their first jobs (Law 456/1951), given at ministry training sectors (though the 1948 Constitution assigned responsibility to the regions), alongside evening classes, courses for apprentices and further training for adults. By 1965, the preliminary training courses, generally lasting two years, had first-year enrolments which were comparable to those of the vocational institutes, each representing around 8 per cent of the relevant age group; in terms of total numbers, the regional courses were much well less placed, as the second-year enrolments were far lower. These streams supplemented the Education Ministry courses, on which they in fact drew substantially, enabling large numbers of young people to obtain qualifications and enter employment.

Another salient feature in the development of the education system was the influence, and considerable magnetism, of the university. As in many other countries, one part of the system was designed, from middle school onwards, not as an end in itself but as preparation for university. At the turn of the century, when enrolment in elementary schools was still very low, Italy had as many university students, in proportion to its population, as other European countries. In 1901, Italy ranked second in this respect, after Germany but ahead of France, Belgium and the Netherlands (Barbagli, 1974). As a percentage of the age cohort, the figure was admittedly modest, but the system's configuration fostered its expansion. It will be seen that today, in terms of university admissions, Italy ranks among the leaders, and may indeed be the world leader. The trend was boosted by an idea strongly held in Italy in the 1960s, that higher education should become "democratic": this meant that, in the name of the right to education and equality of opportunity, university admission should be as open as possible. As in many other countries, this well intentioned idea has also brought an increase in the number of students dropping out.

This brief overview has indicated the broad outlines of the education system in Italy. Before tackling various aspects of its current state, it may be useful to consider what, retrospectively, seem to have been its strengths and weaknesses in the 1960s.

Our observation relates to the selectiveness of the system, which is often attributed to its configuration or the nature of the courses; however, it may equally be due to social expectations at the time. In 1964, school enrolment of 11-14 year-olds (for compulsory schooling) totalled only around 80 per cent (OECD, 1969). Even that figure may present an over-optimistic picture, because just 45 per cent of a cohort actually obtained the certificate marking the end of compulsory schooling. 40 per cent went into the second cycle, but there was a substantial drop-out rate – over half of entrants did not continue to the final diploma, *maturità*. The universities in turn were – even then – shedding two-thirds of their enrolments. We do not think that too much importance should be attached to these drop-outs, because that might lead us to overlook a far more significant and positive aspect, the pace of expansion over this period. Yet when we look at the system's "coverage", in other words the proportion of young people with an opportunity to obtain a post-compulsory qualification, the figure can be put, for 1964-65, at 46 per cent of the cohort, to which can be added 8 per cent for Labour Ministry courses and a few percentage points for apprenticeships. At best, we reach some 56-57 per cent. Nearly half of all young people were not catered for.

## CURRENT TRENDS

There are two dominant, and apparently contradictory, trends today: lower student numbers, except in the lyceums and a few other courses, on account of population decline; and very swift expansion of enrolment in the second cycle of secondary education. The growth in demand is not matched by comparable growth in numbers.

The demographic trend has a direct impact on the compulsory segments, although the number of entrants to elementary education picked up slightly from 1994 onwards. But the impact is clearest in the second cycle of secondary education: between 1990 and 1996 the number of new entrants to the second cycle fell by 14 per cent, even though the proportion moving from the first cycle to the second rose from 86 to 96 per cent. At the same time, the major aspect of the current changes is the expansion of enrolment in the second cycle. Table 2 shows how quickly this has occurred. In particular it can be seen that the proportion of a cohort obtaining the *maturità* rose from 38 to 51 per cent between 1980 and 1990 and then, in just five years, from 51 to 67 per cent between 1990 and 1995. Despite these changes, the number of university entrants is slightly down, partly on account of population trends and partly because the proportion transferring to university has held steady or declined. The picture is thus ambivalent, with some downward trends perhaps concealing substantial expansion.

Table 2. **Percentages of students in full-time education**

|  | 1980 | 1990 | 1995 |
|---|---|---|---|
| Students in second cycle education | 52 | 68 | 80 |
| Students obtaining *maturità*[1] | 38 | 51 | 67 |
| Students enrolled in university[1] | 26 | 36 | 46 |
| Students in university education | 25 | 31 | 40 |

1. As a proportion of the corresponding age cohort.
*Source:* ISFOL (1997a).

These overall trends cover a variety of developments in particular courses. Table 3 shows the breakdown of entrants to second-cycle secondary courses, largely reflecting changing preferences among young people and their families, particularly so at a time when numbers are falling. It reveals expansion in lyceums and the declining attraction of the technical and vocational institutes.

Table 3. **Breakdown of entrants to second-cycle streams**

|  | 1980 | 1985 | 1990 | 1995 | 1996 |
|---|---|---|---|---|---|
| Vocational institutes | 24.2 | 23.1 | 22.8 | 21.5 | 21.1 |
| Technical institutes | 41.6 | 44.0 | 42.2 | 38.1 | 36.9 |
| Lyceums | 20.6 | 21.7 | 24.1 | 27.2 | 27.8 |
| Teacher training | 11.0 | 7.9 | 7.2 | 8.4 | 8.5 |
| Art lyceums and colleges | 2.6 | 3.3 | 3.8 | 3.9 | 5.0 |

*Source:* ISFOL (1997*a*). For 1985: *Thema* (1997).

It is hard to draw any long-term conclusions from these findings; on several occasions in the past trends have reversed, especially between the industrial technical institute and the science lyceum. But the current trend fits a general one in OECD countries (with one or two exceptions), *i.e.* postponing preparation for work to post-secondary level – something for which the systems' structure is not always suited. It may also be thought that in Italy the prestige of the technical institute diploma is starting to wane: even quite recently, as noted, this certificate had a strong image in a context of low school enrolment, but it is less attractive now that two-thirds of young people obtain the *maturità*.

What is lacking from the table is the proportion of young people opting for regional vocational courses. The figures are not always easy to determine because of the wide range of courses available in regional institutions. From 1994, ISTAT has recorded the numbers of entrants to post-compulsory courses (ISTAT, 1996). The flow is round four-fifths of the number of entrants to vocational institutes. While inflows to vocational institutes are slightly down in relative terms, the inflow to regional training is slightly up (ISFOL, 1997*a*). In fact, looking back to the 1965 figures, it can be seen that both tracks have moved largely in parallel up to the present.

At post-secondary level, it may first be noted that the number of entrants to the *laurea* stream has been declining for several years, falling from 334 000 in 1992 to 304 000 in 1996 (MURST, 1997), despite the rapidly rising proportions of each cohort obtaining the *maturità* (Table 2). Demographic reasons supply part of the explanation, but there has also been a fall in transfers to university, down from 71.3 per cent in 1990 to 68.4 per cent in 1995. These figures have moved similarly at other periods, such as the late 1970s, and the decline in demand seems to be linked to a decline in employment opportunities.

Today the *laurea* offers no great advantage in terms of jobs and remuneration (see Section 3 below), and the course is lengthy and the failure rate very high. With enrolment currently over 45 per cent of the cohort, it may be thought (or indeed hoped) that this trend will continue. At the same time, the risk of unemployment needs to be borne in mind; it is highest for young people leaving secondary schooling, who thus have an incentive to enrol in higher education. But the *diploma universitario* stream, recently established,[4] is expanding strongly (see ISFOL, 1997*b*). Enrolments rose from 16 700 in 1992-93 to 28 000 in 1996-97. Numbers expanded by 25 per cent in 1995 and 15 per cent in 1996, and this stream probably now represents one-tenth of inflows to university education. Another expanding sector at post-secondary level is the *post-diploma* courses organised by regional authorities for students with the *maturità*, with 52 000 entrants in 1994-95 (ISTAT, 1996). In 1994-95, around 500 000 students obtained the *maturità*: 64 per cent went into the *laurea* stream, 4 per cent into the *diploma universitario* stream, and 11 per cent into regional *post-diploma* courses. More recent data were not available, but the likely picture is a decline in the first stream and a marked increase in the other two.

One major cause of concern in Italy is the high rate of drop-out, particularly in the second cycle of secondary education and in university courses, although the proportion of students failing to complete compulsory education is now very small (ISFOL puts the proportion not obtaining the *licenza media* at around 5 per cent).

As Table 4 shows, in the second cycle of secondary schooling, students largely drop out in the first and second years. Looking at the trends in enrolment rates based on age alone (see Table 6), the number of students leaving becomes significant between 16 and 17. Student behaviour does not conform with the way educational cycles are organised (ISFOL, 1996 and 1997*a*).

Table 4.  **Drop-out and "survival" rates, by course year, 1992-93**

|  | 1° | 2° | 3° | 4° | 5° |
|---|---|---|---|---|---|
| **Drop-out rate** | | | | | |
| Total | 14.4 | 7.7 | 8.2 | 6.0 | 2.0 |
| Vocational institutes | 21.4 | 10.4 | 9.1 | 12.7[1] | 1.4 |
| Technical institutes | 15.1 | 9.0 | 9.8 | 4.9 | 2.8 |
| Lyceums | 6.7 | 3.3 | 5.3 | 1.9 | 1.0 |
| Others | 13.9 | 8.7 | 6.3 | 10.5 | –[2] |
| **Survival rate** | | | | | |
| Total | 85.6 | 79.0 | 72.5 | 68.2 | 66.8 |
| Vocational institutes | 78.6 | 70.4 | 64.0 | 55.9[1] | 55.1 |
| Technical institutes | 84.9 | 77.3 | 69.7 | 66.3 | 64.4 |
| Lyceums | 93.3 | 90.2 | 85.4 | 83.8 | 83.0 |
| Others | 86.1 | 78.6 | 73.7 | 65.9 | –[2] |

1. At the end of the third year students obtain the *qualifica* and may break off their studies.
2. These courses last four years.
Source:  Micali (1996).

Drop-out and "survival" rates are not the same across all streams. Table 4 shows that the lyceums have the lowest drop-out rates, and the vocational institutes the highest.

The "productivity" of the system varies from one region to another. Table 5 shows that central Italy has the highest proportion of students obtaining the *maturità*; the figures are lower in the North and South. The discrepancy is not all that great, though it is tending to widen slightly. A detailed examination shows a more complex picture, in fact. The regions with the lowest rates are in the North-West (Val d'Aosta) and North-East (Trentino-Alto-Adige), and in Puglia and the Islands (CENSIS, 1996). Piedmont and Lombardy are appreciably below the countrywide average, and below the average for the South. Accordingly, the older typologies do not properly reflect the state of affairs at present. Another development, which may not be new but has come to the fore recently, concerns "returns" to the education system, either during a course or at examination time. ISFOL estimates that, in 1994-95, 13 per cent of second-cycle students dropped out but resumed their courses later on (ISFOL, 1997a).

Table 5. **Enrolment in the first year of the second cycle (for 14-year-olds) (1994)**
**Maturità awards (for 18-year-olds) (1993)**

(percentages by region)

|  | North | Centre | South/Islands | Italy |
|---|---|---|---|---|
| Enrolments | 89.7 | 100.2 | 87.0 | 90.3 |
| Maturità | 56.6 | 66.8 | 53.6 | 57.2 |

Source:    Micali (1996).

We consider that it is important to stress that the "productivity" – in terms of completion rates – of the second cycle of secondary schooling is rising rapidly, which may be due to the trend to extend education, noted in all countries, and perhaps also in part to the job situation for young people. According to ISFOL, the productivity rate was 58 per cent in 1980 and 65 per cent in 1990; it rose to 72 per cent in 1994 and 74 per cent in 1995. In our view this is due to changes in demand rather than changes in teaching practice. We have no information indicating that the second-cycle requirements of schools are being relaxed. We did however note that the pass rate for the *maturità* is 98 per cent among internal candidates, which we felt was really very high; we understand why some of those with whom we spoke suggested that the aim was to see that everyone gets this certificate. That is no doubt an area for investigation as regards the quality of education. It may also be noted that drop-out rates are falling appreciably at secondary level.

Table 6. **Participation rates by age (1995)**

| | School leaving age | Age at end of upper secondary cycle | Net rate for each age (as %) | | | | | | | | | |
|---|---|---|---|---|---|---|---|---|---|---|---|---|
| | | | 15 | 16 | 17 | 18 | 19 | 20 | 21 | 22 | 23 | 24 |
| **North America** | | | | | | | | | | | | |
| Canada | 16 | 17 | **98** | 94 | 79 | 62 | 53 | 57 | 38 | 32 | 24 | 18 |
| Mexico | 15 | 17 | 52 | 39 | 37 | 25 | 15 | 14 | 12 | 10 | 9 | 9 |
| United States | 17 | 17 | **98** | **90** | 79 | 56 | 42 | 35 | 35 | 25 | 23 | 21 |
| **Pacific Area** | | | | | | | | | | | | |
| Australia | 15 | 19 | 98 | 96 | 94 | 66 | 53 | 47 | 34 | 26 | 22 | 20 |
| Japan | 15 | 17 | 101 | 97 | 94 | . . | . . | . . | . . | . . | . . | . . |
| Korea | 14 | 17 | 93 | 95 | 90 | 54 | 42 | 36 | 31 | 23 | 18 | 15 |
| New Zealand | 16 | 17 | **97** | 100 | 77 | 57 | 48 | 45 | 51 | 26 | 19 | 15 |
| **European Union** | | | | | | | | | | | | |
| Austria | 17 | 17-18 | <u>**97**</u> | <u>**94**</u> | 88 | 62 | 36 | 26 | 22 | 18 | 16 | . . |
| Belgium | 18 | 17-19 | <u>**103**</u> | <u>**103**</u> | <u>**100**</u> | 87 | 75 | 67 | 49 | 38 | 28 | 20 |
| Denmark | 16 | 19-20 | **98** | 94 | 82 | 72 | 55 | 42 | 40 | 36 | 33 | 28 |
| Finland | 16 | 17-18 | **99** | 93 | 90 | 81 | 41 | 43 | 49 | 44 | 39 | 32 |
| France | 16 | 17-19 | **98** | 96 | 93 | 84 | 70 | 56 | 42 | 31 | 21 | 13 |
| Germany | 18 | 18 | **99** | <u>**97**</u> | <u>**94**</u> | 84 | 65 | 45 | 34 | 41 | 20 | 18 |
| Greece | 14.5 | 16-18 | 86 | 79 | 56 | 48 | 45 | 36 | 29 | 17 | 13 | 8 |
| Ireland | 15 | 17-18 | 96 | 91 | 81 | 73 | 47 | 37 | 20 | 15 | 13 | 11 |
| Italy | 14 | 19 | 88 | 83 | 75 | 68 | 54 | 39 | 33 | 28 | 24 | 20 |
| Luxembourg | 15 | 17-19 | 80 | 81 | 78 | 70 | . . | . . | . . | . . | . . | . . |
| Netherlands | 18 | 18-19 | **99** | <u>**98**</u> | <u>**93**</u> | 83 | 70 | 60 | 48 | 38 | 30 | 23 |
| Portugal | 14 | 17 | 88 | 73 | 73 | 55 | 45 | 44 | 47 | 25 | 22 | 17 |
| Spain | 16 | 15-17 | **94** | 83 | 75 | 63 | 53 | 50 | 40 | 34 | 25 | 17 |
| Sweden | 16 | 18 | **96** | 97 | 96 | 88 | 35 | 31 | 31 | 30 | 28 | 24 |
| United Kingdom | 16 | 17 | **98** | 87 | 75 | 54 | 45 | 39 | 33 | 22 | 17 | 14 |
| **Other OECD countries** | | | | | | | | | | | | |
| Czech Republic | 15 | 17-19 | 99 | 97 | 72 | 42 | 26 | 20 | 20 | 18 | 11 | 5 |
| Hungary | 16 | 15-17 | **93** | 88 | 71 | 46 | 30 | 25 | 18 | 15 | 12 | 8 |
| Iceland | . . | 19 | . . | 89 | 77 | 65 | 64 | 43 | 38 | 37 | 33 | 27 |
| Norway | 16 | 18 | **100** | 95 | 90 | 83 | 49 | 43 | 41 | 38 | 34 | 27 |
| Poland | 15 | 17-19 | . . | . . | . . | . . | . . | . . | . . | . . | . . | . . |
| Switzerland | 15 | 17-19 | 98 | 87 | 84 | 77 | 57 | 34 | 25 | 21 | 19 | 17 |
| Turkey | 14 | 17-18 | 48 | 40 | 26 | 17 | 17 | 12 | 11 | 10 | 8 | 6 |
| **Country mean** | **16** | **17-18** | **93** | **88** | **79** | **64** | **47** | **39** | **33** | **27** | **21** | **17** |

Notes: . . = Data not available. Figures in bold indicate ages at which schooling is compulsory. Figures underlined indicate ages at which schooling is compulsory at least part-time.
Source: OECD (1997), Table C3.1. For Italy, ISFOL from ISTAT and DOXA data.

Drop-out rates are especially high at universities. This is a well debated issue (see for istance Moortgat, 1996). Italy probably tops the league in the proportion of a given cohort enrolling at university; but it undoubtedly tops the league for the drop-out rate as well and, what is more, since 1990, the figures have been on the rise. According to ISFOL, the universities' productivity rate fell from 36.8 per cent in 1990 to 32.9 per cent in 1995. Failure on this scale would not be of great concern if universities were reserved for the few; but three out of ten of those young Italians who go to university drop out within two or three years. This represents a far more serious problem than the dropping out in the second cycle of the secondary system. The *diploma universitario* courses also have a high drop-out rate, over 50 per cent, and apparently on the increase. This calls for a radical review as soon as possible.

This rapid survey shows strong growth in social demand, apparent so far chiefly in the secondary cycle, with few repercussions as yet at post-secondary level, in spite of the extent of unemployment. This growth has occurred against a virtually unchanged institutional backdrop. The chief innovations have been the occupational *maturità* course, following on from the *qualifica*, in 1969, and the *diploma universitario* course in 1990. Reference should also be made to the changes introduced via experimentation, especially in technical and occupational education, and the developments in regional training, especially at *post-diploma* level. The rise in demand clearly makes some adjustment in the structures of secondary education necessary; but in our view it is even more pressing to consider the structures at post-secondary level, because the *diploma universitario* courses and regional training options are far from matching foreseeable requirements. The creation of a non-university tertiary sector is of cardinal importance.

## EDUCATION AND EMPLOYMENT

Our visit to Italy revealed a wide range of social and economic situations: in some places extraordinary activity and vigour, elsewhere fewer initiatives and narrow horizons. It is true that we visited particularly prosperous northern regions. Our visit to Campania showed us a very much less favourable environment. It is quite likely that we would find equally unfavourable conditions in other provinces or districts, even in the North, whereas there are other areas where unemployment might be termed negative, where workers are rare and where employers are ready to "poach"[5] staff from rival firms by offering them higher wages.

We are aware of the concerns in Italy over employment: economic growth – which in fact slackened in 1996 – is not creating enough jobs to cut back unemployment, and forecasts on this score are guarded. The rate of unemployment is continuing to rise. In the first quarter of 1998 it stood at just over 12 per cent. But these are figures for Italy as a whole. The jobs crisis is particularly acute in the South. Between April 1995 and April 1996 unemployment actually fell a little in the North, but it increased sharply in the South, especially among first-time job seekers. In the spring of 1997 unemployment was 6.7 per cent in the North, 10.7 per cent in central Italy and 22.5 per cent in the South.

Table 7. **Percentage of upper secondary students enrolled in public and private general and vocational education (1995)**

| | General programmes | Vocational and technical programmes | of which: school-based | of which: school and work-based |
|---|---|---|---|---|
| **North America** | | | | |
| Canada | .. | .. | .. | .. |
| Mexico | 83 | 17 | 17 | ● |
| United States | .. | .. | .. | .. |
| **Pacific Area** | | | | |
| Australia | 35 | 65 | ■ | ■ |
| Japan | 72 | 28 | 28 | ● |
| Korea | 57 | 43 | 43 | ○ |
| New Zealand | 62 | 38 | 26 | 12 |
| **European Union** | | | | |
| Austria | 23 | 77 | 42 | 36 |
| Belgium | 32 | 68 | 65 | 3 |
| Denmark | 46 | 54 | ■ | ■ |
| Finland | 48 | 52 | 49 | 3 |
| France | 47 | 53 | 43 | 10 |
| Germany | 23 | 77 | 24 | 53 |
| Greece | 71 | 29 | 29 | ● |
| Ireland | 79 | 21 | 16 | 5 |
| Italy | 28 | 72 | 72 | ● |
| Luxembourg | 36 | 64 | ■ | ■ |
| Netherlands | 30 | 70 | 47 | 23 |
| Portugal | 76 | 24 | 24 | ● |
| Spain | 60 | 40 | 38 | 2 |
| Sweden | 44 | 53 | ■ | ■ |
| United Kingdom | 42 | 58 | ■ | ■ |
| **Other OECD countries** | | | | |
| Czech Republic | 16 | 84 | 36 | 49 |
| Hungary | 27 | 73 | 46 | 27 |
| Iceland | 64 | 36 | 31 | 5 |
| Norway | 45 | 55 | ■ | ■ |
| Poland | .. | .. | .. | .. |
| Switzerland | 31 | 69 | 9 | 61 |
| Turkey | 56 | 44 | 44 | ■ |
| **Country mean** | **47** | **53** | **37** | **17** |

Notes:  ● = Data not available because the category does not apply; .. = Data not available; ○ = Magnitude is either negligible or zero; ■ = Data included in another category/column of the table.
Source:   OECD (1997), Table C3.2..

Another feature of the employment situation in Italy is the high level of youth unemployment, the highest in Europe after Spain, amounting to 32.6 per cent of 20- to 24-year-olds in 1995 (see Table 8). There is nothing new about this: we identified the characteristic back in the 1970s. At the time we attributed it largely to the very high level of job protection in Italy, which places the burden of unemployment on those on the fringes of the labour market, young people and also women, whose participation rate is rising. Long-term unemployment is substantially youth unemployment. These factors combine to produce very high jobless rates: in the south, around 50 per cent for 15- to 24-year-olds (against 18 per cent elsewhere) and 65 per cent for women (ISFOL, 1997a).

The OECD *Economics Survey* highlights the progress that has been made in improving labour market flexibility, but it seems that greater flexibility is attributable more to changes in working practices which did not necessarily imply open-ended employment contracts than to any fundamental shift. As far as young people are concerned, our interviews confirmed that a whole range of devices, such as work-experience courses, employment-training contracts, apprenticeships, part-time working, "co-ordinated and on-going collaboration" and "consulting" (ISFOL, 1996), were used to avoid long-term recruitment.

A further feature of employment in Italy (which is also found in Greece and Portugal, but not in quite the same way in Spain) is that the unemployment rate among young people rises with the level of qualification (see Table 8). Among 20- to 24-year-olds, the rate is 27.6 per cent for those with qualifications lower than *maturità*, rising to 37.6 per cent for those with secondary diplomas and 38.5 per cent for those with university degrees. The corresponding figures for the 25-29 age bracket are 16.6 per cent, 17.3 per cent and 32.7 per cent. A special ISTAT study (ISTAT, 1997) found that this was partly due to the fact that students graduate very late and start looking for work when others of similar age are already in stable situations. CENSIS estimates that *laureati* take an average of 19 months to find work (CENSIS, 1996). A counter-example would be those young people in the north who drop out of higher education before completing their courses because they have already found work.

We also listened to what employers had to say (as well as reading numerous articles in the press and in specialist publications). First, employers regretted that young people were not interested in the jobs offered to them, especially in the manufacturing sector. One suggested reason was that they were badly advised or badly informed about the nature of such jobs in modern industry.[6] Another reason often mentioned was that they were less interested in the work than in the pay. That is not necessarily a cause for worry over *il malessere del benessere*, meaning young people are in some way cursed with a fullness of blessings. It may be supposed – or hoped – that maturity will come later, with the experience of work.

Table 8. **Youth unemployment rates
by level of educational attainment and age group (1995)**

| | Below upper secondary education | | | Upper secondary education | | | Non-university tertiary education | | University-level education | | All levels of education | | |
|---|---|---|---|---|---|---|---|---|---|---|---|---|---|
| | Age 15-19 | Age 20-24 | Age 25-29 | Age 15-19 | Age 20-24 | Age 25-29 | Age 20-24 | Age 25-29 | Age 20-24 | Age 25-29 | Age 15-19 | Age 20-24 | Age 25-29 |
| **North America** | | | | | | | | | | | | | |
| Canada | 21.3 | 25.6 | 19.5 | 14.6 | 12.9 | 11.7 | 10.9 | 8.8 | 8.6 | 5.4 | 18.2 | 13.7 | 10.2 |
| Mexico | .. | .. | .. | .. | .. | .. | .. | .. | .. | .. | .. | .. | .. |
| United States | 20.4 | 19.4 | 13.3 | 10.2 | 9.1 | 7.0 | 5.4 | 3.7 | 3.9 | 3.0 | 16.9 | 9.5 | 6.2 |
| **Pacific Area** | | | | | | | | | | | | | |
| Australia | 23.0 | 16.4 | 11.9 | 17.4 | 10.9 | 7.5 | 9.8 | 4.4 | 6.5 | 4.7 | 21.0 | 12.0 | 8.4 |
| Japan | .. | .. | .. | .. | .. | .. | .. | .. | .. | .. | .. | .. | .. |
| Korea | 8.9 | 4.5 | 2.7 | 7.6 | 5.3 | 2.6 | ■ | ■ | 9.0 | 3.8 | 7.9 | 5.9 | 3.0 |
| New Zealand | 17.7 | 16.1 | 11.1 | 10.8 | 5.6 | 3.2 | 6.4 | 5.5 | 3.5 | 2.9 | 15.7 | 8.1 | 5.8 |
| **European Union** | | | | | | | | | | | | | |
| Austria | 6.4 | 7.6 | 7.2 | 4.9 | 3.9 | 3.1 | 3.6 | 2.1 | 0.8 | 3.6 | 5.9 | 4.5 | 3.8 |
| Belgium | 22.9 | 29.7 | 18.9 | 27.3 | 19.2 | 11.1 | 9.7 | 4.8 | 14.5 | 5.7 | 25.3 | 20.0 | 10.7 |
| Denmark | 3.3 | 18.4 | 21.7 | 7.4 | 9.3 | 8.3 | 14.2 | 6.6 | 9.9 | 7.7 | 3.7 | 12.9 | 12.1 |
| Finland | 30.6 | 41.6 | 32.0 | 38.9 | 26.2 | 18.5 | 23.1 | 16.2 | 20.6 | 9.4 | 33.6 | 29.1 | 19.4 |
| France | 25.3 | 41.3 | 27.6 | 23.2 | 24.8 | 15.0 | 18.9 | 8.4 | 14.4 | 13.8 | 24.4 | 26.1 | 15.3 |
| Germany | 5.6 | 12.5 | 15.5 | 7.5 | 6.8 | 6.9 | 4.7 | 4.9 | .. | 5.1 | 7.2 | 8.1 | 7.7 |
| Greece | 25.7 | 17.8 | 12.6 | 50.4 | 30.9 | 16.4 | 39.8 | 18.1 | 42.6 | 21.4 | 35.2 | 28.4 | 16.4 |
| Ireland | 35.2 | 28.7 | 23.5 | 21.6 | 12.2 | 8.4 | 8.8 | 6.4 | 9.0 | 5.4 | 28.2 | 16.0 | 12.0 |
| Italy | 34.6 | 27.6 | 16.6 | 47.8 | 37.6 | 17.3 | ■ | ■ | 38.5 | 32.7 | 37.7 | 32.6 | 18.2 |
| Luxembourg | 15.0 | 9.6 | 5.9 | 18.8 | 4.8 | 2.8 | ■ | ■ | 14.9 | 0.6 | 15.2 | 9.1 | 4.6 |
| Netherlands | 19.0 | 13.4 | 9.2 | 15.0 | 7.4 | 5.5 | ● | ● | 12.0 | 7.6 | 18.2 | 9.9 | 7.0 |
| Portugal | 16.1 | 14.2 | 8.9 | 34.2 | 20.1 | 9.8 | 22.7 | 9.9 | 14.5 | 10.3 | 17.2 | 15.6 | 9.2 |
| Spain | 49.6 | 37.4 | 32.3 | 54.3 | 41.0 | 27.2 | 40.4 | 23.7 | 53.1 | 33.2 | 50.6 | 39.8 | 30.4 |
| Sweden | 19.6 | 30.0 | 21.3 | 24.2 | 18.9 | 12.2 | 10.6 | 6.1 | 8.1 | 7.5 | 20.9 | 19.2 | 11.6 |
| United Kingdom | 28.1 | 31.8 | 27.8 | 14.9 | 13.2 | 9.8 | 5.6 | 4.4 | 12.2 | 3.7 | 17.3 | 14.2 | 10.1 |
| **Other OECD countries** | | | | | | | | | | | | | |
| Czech Republic | 24.8 | 18.6 | 17.2 | 9.0 | 3.1 | 3.4 | ■ | ■ | 2.2 | 0.7 | 13.0 | 4.0 | 4.0 |
| Hungary | .. | .. | .. | .. | .. | .. | .. | .. | .. | .. | .. | .. | .. |
| Iceland | .. | .. | .. | .. | .. | .. | .. | .. | .. | .. | .. | .. | .. |
| Norway | 16.9 | 18.3 | 14.4 | 14.4 | 10.0 | 6.8 | 8.3 | 6.5 | 7.0 | 4.0 | 15.8 | 10.3 | 6.9 |
| Poland | 30.6 | 32.0 | 26.1 | 50.8 | 26.7 | 14.4 | 26.0 | 8.8 | 17.2 | 7.4 | 44.2 | 27.1 | 14.5 |
| Switzerland | 18.0 | ■ | ■ | ■ | 4.6 | 3.5 | ■ | 1.6 | ■ | 4.2 | 16.0 | 5.8 | 4.1 |
| Turkey | 10.9 | 12.3 | 8.0 | 32.9 | 23.9 | 12.4 | ■ | ■ | 29.7 | 7.8 | 13.8 | 16.1 | 8.9 |
| **Country mean** | **21.2** | **21.9** | **16.9** | **23.3** | **15.5** | **9.8** | **14.9** | **7.9** | **15.3** | **8.5** | **20.9** | **15.9** | **10.4** |

Notes: ● = Data not available because the category does not apply; .. = Data not available; ■ = Data included in another category/column of the table.
Source: OECD (1997), Table E3.1.

Employers' criticisms of youth training come as no surprise either. The most frequent remark was that it is impossible to find skilled technicians.[7] While it is true that enrolments at technical and vocational institutes are down, in both comparative and absolute terms, Italy's education system produces a proportion of graduates with such skills (see Table 7). Even if some young people continue their studies, even if the proportion of industrial certificates is down slightly (representing a quarter of technical institute students, a little over a third of vocational institute students), it cannot be said that Italy does not train skilled people. Other parameters must be brought in, notably the type of demand by some firms.

It is more difficult to summarise the other comments we heard. There is a general consensus in favour of a higher level of education, a better technical general culture and "transverse" skills, meaning broader-based education and training. At the same time, however, there is a demand for more highly specialised training that keeps abreast of new equipment and new technology. It is also generally agreed that priority should be given to "mid-level" qualifications, meaning qualifications that are higher than the traditional vocational qualification (the *qualifica*) and are thus at *maturità* or post-secondary level.[8] Lastly, there is general agreement on the need for greater flexibility. However, disagreements and even contradictions begin to appear when it comes to identifying the right combination of these elements and the means of achieving it.

And yet the issue is an important one when there is a proposal to introduce an "integrated system" which affects all the parties concerned. We know that large firms as a rule want broad-based training, preferring to train specialist staff themselves, whereas small and medium-sized businesses need ready-trained specialists because they generally do not have the resources to do their own training. It is equally true that many large firms are drastically cutting their training budgets and that it is sometimes in small and medium-sized businesses that the level and quality of training are highest. In many cases also, specialist small firms are the only ones able to provide young people with the necessary training, which sometimes requires lengthy apprenticeship. Moreover, some firms cover an entire manufacturing process and want a majority of semi-skilled or unskilled workers while others carry out only assembly work and are looking for technicians responsible for starting and controlling processes.

We took a particular interest in the situation in Italy because of the high proportion of small businesses (in 1994, companies with less than 50 employees represented almost 90 per cent of the total number of companies and 40 per cent of salaried employment, excluding the primary sector and domestic services) and self-employed workers (almost 30 per cent of total employment) (ISFOL, 1996).

# 3

# REFORMING THE SCHOOL SYSTEM

Having outlined some thoughts on the state of education in Italy, in this chapter we shall examine issues relating to the proposed reforms. On this point, we wish to emphasise that we are unable to consider all the issues currently under discussion in educational circles in Italy. We have to choose those that we regard as crucial and on which we believe we can usefully comment from an external perspective.

The reform proposals constitute a vast undertaking in which all the elements are linked. It is difficult to discuss one aspect without others coming to mind. Consequently, it was not easy to define the structure of this report. We have decided to devote this chapter to reform of the school system. We will begin with curriculum reform; we will then consider the reform of educational cycles and the issues it raises; before discussing the current status and future of the teaching profession.[9]

## THE NATURE AND SPIRIT OF THE CURRICULUM

In seeking to understand the reasons which led the Italian government to embark on a complete overhaul of the education system, we believe that we have managed to identify a certain number of central ideas, alongside which the others are purely instrumental. We felt that one of these fundamental ideas originated in current reactions to the exponential growth of knowledge, the spread of increasingly advanced technologies, and the transformation of the world. A new culture is emerging, raising questions about the knowledge and skills that all children should acquire. Consequently, the minister set up a special commission – *Commissione dei Saggi* – given the task of determining "the basic knowledge that young people should acquire in Italian schools in the coming decades" (Commissione dei Saggi, 1997). The preamble to the draft framework law on the reform of educational cycles (*disegno di legge quadro in materia di riordino dei cicli d'istruzione*) makes explicit reference to the commission's work.

### The work of the *Commissione dei Saggi*

The commission identified a certain number of areas where the curriculum needed to be brought up to date. Some are of a very general nature, such as the identity of the individual to be educated, the Italian identity in Europe and the world, education in democracy, civic responsibility and sustainable development. Others concern the prevailing culture in schools, the over-emphasis on cognitive and verbal skills and the lack of importance given to practical skills, the nature of the links between schools and the workplace. Yet others relate more directly to teaching, including the structure of curricula in view of the proliferation of sources of information and methods of learning. The commission's discussions have been highly instructive, though of necessity couched in rather general and philosophical terms. They are currently being continued in the *Accademia dei Lincei*, which has been asked to consider the conclusions that can be drawn from the commission's work as regards the organisation and nature of the curriculum.

It is clear that although some of the commission's conclusions are drawn from its reflections on the new culture, others derive from a comparison between these reflections and the current state of Italian education. The report summarising their work[10] contains a number of direct and indirect criticisms of the spirit and content of the current school curriculum. While it is not our place to join in these criticisms, we can point out that much of the criticism directed at the school and university culture corresponds to trends that may be found in many other countries. Education, so the argument goes, ought to instil values, arouse interest and curiosity, develop taste and lead to a certain level of independence and self-control through reading, writing, the arts and manual work. Instead it is sinking into abstraction, concentrating on dry book-learning and the memorisation of facts, turning out young people who, according to some criteria, know a great deal and are capable of achieving high marks in exams but have not learnt how to think, have failed to acquire any culture. Moreover, there is an ever-present tendency to add new subjects and expand the scope of existing ones. Confronted with over-inflated curricula, the most pupils can do is to try and memorise a few important elements. We thoroughly endorse the basic tenet of the reform, namely to switch from a style of education that overemphasises the transmission of knowledge to one that encourages reflection and experiment and facilitates the acquisition and integration of knowledge and skills. The preamble to the framework law rightly emphasises the fact that these two approaches to learning are complementary.

The work of the commission continues, and conclusions will have to be drawn as regards the various levels and sectors of the education system. Schools will have to develop a culture of greater independence and responsibility and approach education from a new standpoint. At this stage, the best we can do is to offer a few brief remarks.

## Lifelong learning

Italy, along with other OECD countries, is seeking to integrate the notion of lifelong learning into educational policy-making since the pace of change in job and skill requirements makes lifelong learning an imperative. The flexibility that results from decentralisation should make it possible to pay more attention to lifelong learning in the context of the reforms.

Above all, teachers in the system must demonstrate their own commitment to lifelong learning by attending in-service training courses and by providing opportunities for people in their region to use school facilities for educational programmes that will contribute to their ongoing learning throughout life. This is no doubt one of the purposes of the directive on the activities of education institutions (Directive 133/1996). Adult education, because it is less threatening and more open, often provides a way for low achievers, or women who have been out of the work force for some time, to embark on an educational programme, perhaps in literacy or numeracy, which can lead to more formal study. A whole range of facilities, such as school buildings after hours, workplace spaces and church halls, can be used for this purpose. The Internet will also increasingly provide a channel for bringing adults the material they need to set them on a path to new knowledge.

Lifelong learning is of course a much broader concept, much discussed at present within the OECD. One of the key issues is its implications for the objectives and content of initial education. The preamble to the draft framework law rightly indicates that initial education should focus on fundamental competencies and the ability to acquire and assimilate new skills and knowledge. This will be the first challenge for those responsible for preparing the new curriculum.

**Key competencies**

One of the main innovations of the reform, linked to the schools' new autonomy, is to define their objectives and the outcomes, particularly in terms of student competencies. Hitherto, the ministry produced detailed curricula for each subject; henceforth, schools and staff will be free to choose the methods by which they intend to bring pupils to a certain level of knowledge.

As countries move from input to output evaluation of their educational progress, from curriculum statements and teacher/student ratios to the issue of what young people need to know at various stages of their development, the expected outcomes should be made explicit by teachers to their pupils, their parents and their potential employers. Arguably, one of the explicit motives for extending compulsory schooling is to ensure that by the time young people leave school they will have acquired the basic competencies they need to function effectively both in the workplace and in the wider community. But what are these basic competencies?

Several OECD countries have identified what they define as the key competencies necessary for working life. Various levels of achievement are defined for each competency and methods have been developed to test them so that parents, employers and the young people themselves can know what skills they have.

Important areas such as communication skills, both written and oral, numeracy skills, computer and technology skills, problem solving and analysis are generally encompassed in some form. Some countries add civics and social skills or multicultural understanding. We regard the lower secondary cycle, to the end of compulsory education, as the best time for focusing on these basic skills and defining the level that each pupil should attain. The Italian authorities are working on a national system for identifying and testing basic skills, in order in particular to evaluate each pupil's attainments at the end of compulsory schooling.

We acknowledge that there is considerable international debate in this area, and some of the work undertaken in the United States, the United Kingdom, Australia and some other countries may be instructive. For example, some experts consider that competencies are context-specific and can be generalised only to a minimal extent; others believe that certain basic principles apply whatever the context, and that hence generalisable competencies can be developed. Key competencies do not constitute a curriculum, but the way the school curriculum is taught should help to develop them. The extent to which learning activities help to develop these competencies should be a fundamental part of curriculum design. It is also important that, in the preparation of curricula, attention be paid to the development of key competencies necessary to cope effectively with future working life, and in particular that these competencies be taken into account in the way the curriculum is taught.

**Technology**

As we have seen, the commission looked at the education issues raised by the spread of information and communication technologies. In addition, the ministry has launched a four-year programme (1997-2000) to develop "teaching technologies". We were able to broach these subjects during our visits.

Education systems are becoming increasingly dependent upon information technology to provide communication tools, a medium for teaching and learning and a channel through which performance can be monitored and information transmitted.

Internet technology is also a cheap and efficient means of communication between schools, making it easier to share expertise, compare data relating to student learning or costs and efficiency, and open up pathways to the world outside the classroom. In order for the system to be monitored closely, it is important for schools to be linked both with each other and with central and regional educational agencies so that data can be transmitted and aggregated quickly and results made available to all who may have a legitimate interest in them.

Some schools we visited had computer facilities but there is still a steep learning curve before they can be used fully and effectively to support educational reform. We are also aware that many schools do not yet have the necessary equipment to contribute effectively to the reform process. This should be a priority, and we believe that individual schools and regions should develop their own strategic plans for enhancing their information technology support. Overall, central government should monitor progress, make its data requirements explicit and ensure that sufficient resources are both made available and applied in order to meet an educational need. This is certainly in line with the ministry's current efforts, but we realise that the framing and implementation of initiatives in this field will present a major challenge.

The Italian authorities attach high importance to these questions and are continuing their efforts, in a planned and systematic way, to make the necessary computer equipment available to every school and develop the necessary networks so that schools can communicate effectively both with each other and with monitoring authorities at various levels, notably with regard to the implementation and evaluation of the reforms. We suggest that a comprehensive in-service training programme be put in place so that information technology may come to be used fully and effectively for teaching, administration and evaluation. It is one thing to provide the equipment; it is quite another for that technology to be used effectively. Considerable effort is needed at all levels if this is to be achieved.

## THE REFORM OF EDUCATION CYCLES

Although the reforms are underpinned by a number of fundamental guiding ideas, such as equity, the equal dignity of various abilities, or the definition of new competencies, there are others that are of a more instrumental nature. Autonomy is doubtless one of these, and the reform of educational cycles certainly is. Yet it is one of the most important planks of the wider systemic reform. It is also the subject of lively debate. This is understandable, since the change in the educational landscape will also affect the lives of hundreds of thousands of pupils and teachers.

Our standpoint is rather different. There is an amazing diversity of education systems in the OECD countries. Yet systems which seem quite different can produce comparable results. Among the most important factors are the content of the curriculum, the way subjects are taught, the quality of schooling and the interface between school and the outside world. Consequently, we feel there is no point joining battle over an issue such as whether a cycle should last three years rather than four. At the same time, we recognise that the world is changing and that a structure which was appropriate thirty years ago is probably no longer suited to the expectations and aspirations of modern society. Experts in what Italians call "structural engineering" (ingegneria strutturale) often emphasise the phases of a child's development. They are right, and research has made much progress in this field. It is logical to want to bring together children who have reached the same stage of development, in the same cycle and in the same educational framework. When age gaps are too great, it is also sometimes desirable to keep children apart. However, there are other arguments to be considered, such as enrolment rates. Just as country roads are ill-suited to urban rush-hour traffic, so an education system designed for the few no longer works when extended to encompass the many. Moreover, society and the economy are evolving. Skill requirements are changing and education, especially technical and vocational training, needs to adapt accordingly.

Any set of proposals for educational reform is bound to raise a certain number of questions, albeit in the knowledge that there will be no single answer. Such questions may relate, for example, to selection, or to the possibilities for progress or further training, or to remedial provision for pupils in difficulty. They could concern the links between general education and vocational training. They could concern what may happen if enrolment rates continue to rise. Lastly, reform raises the question of what will happen to existing institutions, even if only the school buildings, and of course what will happen to teachers. We propose in the following section to comment on various aspects of the reform. We will devote a specific section to teachers later, and the next chapter will look at aspects relating to the organisation of technical and vocational education.

### Compulsory schooling

Diagrams 1 and 2 show the current system and the system proposed by the government. The diagrams have of course been simplified. In the current system, for example, *scuole magistrali* and special purpose schools have not been shown separately. There is also a margin of interpretation. For example, the government project uses the term *"indirizzi"* in the lower secondary cycle but it is by no means certain that this necessarily implies separate streams.

There has been a long-standing debate on the extension of compulsory schooling in Italy which, among the most advanced OECD countries, was the only one to have a school leaving age as low as 14. This could be perceived as one of the contributory factors to Italy's "education gap". Several proposals were brought before Parliament but no agreement was ever reached, not least because some educationalists argued for an extension of the comprehensive system while others wanted to introduce a measure of streaming. More recently, attention has been directed to the reform of the secondary school curriculum. The Brocca Commission, set up in 1988, looked at the curriculum for the two-year lower secondary cycle (*biennio*), to see how common elements could be strengthened both within and between the three main sectors (lyceums, technical and vocational institutes). In the absence of comprehensive reform, a start had been made on developing closer links between these different educational paths, by way of experimental schemes in particular, thus paving the way for an extension of compulsory schooling.

✦  Diagram 1.  **Current system**

Secondary school

Lyceum

Technical institute

Vocational institute

University *(laurea)*

Early childhood education

Elementary school

Comprehensive school

3 ... 6 ... 11 ... 14

Teacher's training school

19

University *(diploma)*

Art institute

FPR, level 1

FPR, level 2

Compulsory schooling

6 ——————————————— 14

✦  Diagram 2.  **System proposed by the government**

Secondary school

*Umanistico*

*Scientifico*

University *(laurea)*

*Tecnico*

University *(diploma)*

Pre-school

Primary school

3 ... 6 ... 12

15

*Tecnologico*

18

Post-secondary education

*Artistico*

FPR, level 1

FPR, level 2

Compulsory schooling

5 ——————————————— 15

*Note:*  FPR = Regional vocational training.
*Source:*  OECD.

The reform proposals call for 10 years compulsory schooling rather than 8, from the ages of five to fifteen, consisting of the last year of pre-school, primary school (six years) and a lower secondary "orientation" cycle (three years). The reasons for this choice are clear. One is to preserve a sufficiently extensive common core, including the last year of pre-school, so as to ensure greater equality of opportunity. Another is to encourage talents and respond to a wide range of interests, through differentiation in the lower secondary cycle. A third is to reduce the total length of the primary plus secondary cycle by lowering the age of *maturità* (comparable projects exist with regard to the length of university cycles). There was also a feeling that it was perhaps premature, if not unnecessary, to raise the school-leaving age to 16, given that a significant proportion of young people already leave school at 15. However that may be, the proposal raises the question of the significance of compulsory schooling at a time when most pupils already pursue their studies well beyond school leaving age.

It is true that compulsory schooling still has a strong symbolic value. It corresponds to a commitment from the state which guarantees all children the possibility of education for a certain number of years. Raising the school leaving age irreversibly consolidates the progress that has been made in getting children to attend school. Even though most young people stay at school beyond leaving age, compulsory schooling is at least a guarantee that the least well-off will receive an education, "whatever its objective effects on the conditions of access to employment and the social recognition accorded to diplomas, qualifications and wages" (Fauroux Commission, 1996).

Wider objectives have been attached to compulsory schooling, such as the construction of a national identity and, more recently, the promotion of greater equality of opportunity (both of which may imply attending a school common to all). It was the latter idea which, in Italy, laid behind the creation of comprehensive middle schools (*scuola media unica*) and other projects such as the extension of the elementary school cycle. But, as we shall see, the results of comprehensive schooling as regards equality of opportunity have not always come up to expectations and the idea of differentiation as a response to the diversity of talents has tempered earlier attitudes.

Under these circumstances compulsory schooling, as the Fauroux Commission has said, "is neither strict in scope nor precise in content, and only its redefinition in terms of an obligation of results can restore these attributes" (Fauroux Commission, 1996). The commission refers to the notion of "basic competencies". This is the broad position adopted in the Italian proposals within a framework of autonomy but, we feel, in a less explicit manner where compulsory schooling in particular is concerned.

It is the responsibility of the state to determine what it will require each young person at the end of compulsory schooling to know and be able to do. It is for the state to prepare young people for their work future knowing that at least legally they can leave school and attempt to enter the work force after the age of 15 years. At the end of compulsory schooling, responsibility shifts: from the government which until then had the right to determine what every young person was to know or do at school, and the right to test whether they have achieved their expectations, to the young person and their families who take over responsibility and determine the path to their likely work future. This requires significant guidance being made available to young people and their families to give them appropriate information about educational and/or work opportunities most suited to their needs and aspirations. This view of compulsory schooling shifts its focus from being an input concept to make sure that young people attend school, to an output concept, where schools on behalf of the state are expected to make sure that each young person has a certain state-determined minimal level of knowledge and skill at the end of their compulsory schooling. The effort is not so much on getting young people to go to school: that occurs now more or less automatically. The effort is now to ensure that they have learned at least a minimal level of knowledge and skill before they leave.

Because of the shift of responsibility from government to individual at the end of compulsory schooling, the age of 15 becomes an important one in testing what children know at the end of 10 years of this period. The profile obtained from such testing becomes very useful in helping young people make decisions about their future, know where their aptitudes lie, and more importantly find out which areas of knowledge and skill require attention if they are to be successful in post-compulsory schooling or work.

Here, the proposals are relatively ambiguous on the subject of how to assess whether pupils have acquired the "basic competencies" or achieved the statutory objectives or standards, and even as to the nature of those standards. As the assessment is based on the schooling common to all, we believe that the certificate or final diploma should relate exclusively to the competencies required of all, a matter to which we shall return.

The reform proposal also provides for a right to education until the age of 18. This idea has already been taken up in a number of OECD countries, especially in northern Europe. The connection between this right to education and the notion of compulsory schooling remains to be defined. We would merely point out that a number of pupils either drop out of school before the end of compulsory schooling (especially if it is extended by a year) or fail to reach the required level before leaving school. For such pupils, we recommend the introduction of individual monitoring, another subject to which we shall return.

## Pre-school

A few years ago the Italian pre-school system hit the international headlines: Italian kindergartens, especially in the Modena and Reggio Emilia regions, had been cited by *Newsweek* magazine as the best in the world. The OECD had already drawn the attention of the international community to these achievements at a seminar on pre-school education at Bologna in 1984.

The reform proposal has the merit of acknowledging the special place of pre-schools and of highlighting their educational importance. Efforts must be made to ensure that existing methods are preserved and that the last year of pre-school does not become a period of school learning. On the contrary, the teaching methods developed in Italian pre-schools should perhaps inspire those of teachers in the first years of primary school. We believe that it is vital first to preserve the difference and specificity of pre-schools and then to see how continuity can be ensured. This could serve as a starting-point for further reflection and research.

The pre-school sector is the one in which the state plays by far the least important role. Non-state elementary schools account for only 8 per cent of pupils, and the proportions in the lower and upper secondary cycles are 4 per cent and 7 per cent respectively (figures for 1995-96). In pre-schools, the proportion is 46 per cent. The reasons for this are historical. In the past, most pre-schools were founded by the Church. Local authorities soon followed their example and in 1968, in order to ensure greater equality of opportunity, state pre-schools were created. At the present time (1996-97), 42.5 per cent of pre-school children are in non-state institutions, with 14 per cent attending local authority schools, 19 per cent church schools and 9 per cent private schools (Ministry of Education, 1997).

In these conditions, making the last year of pre-school compulsory implies first ensuring equal quality and a certain degree of homogeneity across the system. Second, the need to subsidise schools outside the state sector has to be envisaged. On this point, we are aware of the existence of proposals which provide for subsidies in certain cases. There has long been legislation regarding quality, teaching conditions and the qualifications of teachers. It charges *provveditorati* with "vigilance", giving them a duty to monitor the quality of teaching and the right to open or close private, provincial and state schools. However, the extension of compulsory schooling suggests that these measures should be reviewed in order to see whether they correspond to the new requirements that may arise. The implications of this change for staff and their development to cope with the new arrangements will also have to be taken into consideration.

### Primary school

We were struck by the number of teachers and non-teaching staff in the primary schools. The pupil/teaching staff ratio is exceptionally low. According to *Education at a Glance* (1997, Table B8.1), of all the OECD countries the ratio in Italy is the second lowest after Norway: 10.6 in the state sector, 11.0 for the state and private sector as a whole. Thus, there are two teachers for a class of twenty or so children, sometimes a third if there is a handicapped child in the class. Law 148/1990 provides for three teachers for two classes. Under the circumstances, it is hardly surprising that children receive a level of attention rarely encountered in other countries. And yet in the schools we visited traditional teaching methods prevailed, and the organisation of classes was hardly conducive to more active and more modern methods. But we were interested to see that, from the third to the final year of primary school, most children learn a foreign language, the teachers being specially trained for the purpose.

Primary school education has been reformed twice. There was a radical reform of the curriculum in 1985 (DPR 104/1985) and of teaching methods in 1990 (Law 148/1990).These reforms have been monitored and evaluated, and a report to Parliament endorsed their main thrusts. It takes time for such far-reaching reforms to be carried through, especially when they affect almost three million pupils. The essential issue for the reforms is to ensure that children in primary school are well prepared for the next educational cycle and that the transition from primary to secondary education is as smooth as possible.

The reform calls for 6 years of primary schooling, divided into three 2-year cycles. Similar systems have been introduced in many OECD countries and we have no objection to the proposal. As we have seen, the cycle has been reformed twice in recent times and we cannot say whether the reforms have been completed success-fully. It is possible that the number of teachers may have played a role: the recruit-ment of new teachers has continued despite falling school rolls, and the closure of schools which have become too small may well create a fresh surplus.

We assume that the changes in the primary school system are inspired by consid-erations relating to the duration of the common core and the introduction of differenti-ation during compulsory schooling, which we mentioned earlier. On this subject, we are concerned by a point in the preamble which associates objectives of "consolidation, development and extension of acquired knowledge and the ability to work and think autonomously", with the final 2-year cycle of primary school. We acknowledge that add-ing a year to the cycle means that its objective can be broadened, but we are not con-vinced that children between the ages of ten and twelve are capable of consolidating knowledge and acquiring the genuine ability to work and make judgements and choices autonomously. That objective is ambitious enough for the lower secondary cycle. We find the idea an interesting one, admittedly, and we are following its applica-tion attentively; at the same time we invite the Italian authorities to think about ways and means of making headway, in particular in terms of support for teachers.

Another point which we felt deserved attention is the proposal for an "assess-ment" at the end of each 2-year cycle, the final one having the status of a state examination. In order to dispel any ambiguity over the Italian word *valutazione* we would like a clear distinction to be drawn between evaluation, which concerns schools, and assessment, which concerns pupils, since the methods and the purposes of each are different.

We believe that an evaluation every two years could prove onerous if it covered all pupils, and that there should be two at most. But we acknowledge that the proposal would provide more chance for timely intervention. As far as assessment is concerned, it can be a useful diagnostic and remedial tool but should not become a criterion for transition from one 2-year cycle to the next. Lastly, we wonder whether it is really necessary to introduce or keep a state examination at a level which currently marks only one stage among others in a child's progression through the compulsory cycles of the education system, especially as many countries have actually abolished such exams.

### The orientation cycle

The Italian reform proposals once again raise the subject of the single compulsory stream: this is another aspect of their originality. The debate about comprehensive schools was one of the major issues in education in the 1960s. The parties of the left saw comprehensive education, together with a raising of the school leaving age, not only as a way of ensuring greater equality of opportunity but also of achieving greater equality of educational results between social classes. The debate was a lively one, and not all countries adopted the same model of comprehensive education. Some, like Germany, Switzerland, Austria, Netherlands, did not go down the comprehensive road at all (OECD, 1983). In all events, the issue was so politically sensitive that for many years it was difficult to discuss the model's weaknesses and strengths objectively.

Italy had opted for a hard-line position with the *scuola media unica*, though it has been greatly softened in the more recent past by the possibilities opened up by experiments (it must be said, however, that these possibilities have been somewhat chaotic and very different from one school to another and have perhaps reintroduced fresh inequalities between schools or regions). However, these schools have achieved their objective of ensuring that almost all young people attend school up to the age of fourteen. In 1945, the attendance rate of the corresponding age group was 20 per cent; the proportion had risen to 59 per cent by 1962 and reached almost 100 per cent around 1975 (Cecchi, 1997). However, these figures do not mean that all young people complete the educational cycle. Twelve per cent of pupils enrolling in the 3-year *licenza* cycle in 1991 did not actually obtain the diploma in 1994 (CENSIS, 1996, Table 32).

One aspect of the government proposals which aroused our concern, however, was the use of the term *indirizzo*, which is used for the upper secondary and university cycles and implies the choice of a career. We fear that pupils, families and teachers alike could interpret the word in a way which goes well beyond the minister's real intentions. The term *indirizzo* and the paths to which it applies in the body of the draft framework law imply that children will be choosing a particular specialisation at the age of 13 or even 12. The proposals do not specify the scope of the common core and of specialist subjects, but the latter could well represent a third of the total. Our concern is heightened by the fact that the list of *indirizzi* presented is the same as for upper secondary, and the first-cycle certificate allows entry to schools with the same *indirizzo*. We feel that this tree-like structure may be suitable for university, where courses branch out from a common trunk, and then ramify. We do not think it is appropriate for this age group.

We prefer the idea of "options",[11] designed not so as to correspond to second cycle streams but so as to detect, encourage and develop the different interests and abilities of children: mathematics but chess as well; history, but also the restoration and preservation of historical monuments; sport and gymnastics, but also ballet, all taught not in the spirit of academic book-learning but as soon as possible from a practical, concrete, applied standpoint. The idea is one on which there is broad consensus. Several factors encourage us in this approach. First, timetables in Italian schools leave plenty of scope for extra-curricular activities. Second, Directive 133 of 1996 develops the ideas of schools as cultural centres which can accommodate or stimulate various types of activity and of greater integration of schools into the community. Third, we have the impression that throughout Italy there are people, both in schools and in the community, who are capable of awakening and nurturing the most varied abilities and interests.

One interesting idea is not only being able to change options from one year to another (an idea included in the draft framework law) but also and above all of being able to choose two or three options that are as different as possible from one another. The underlying idea, of course, is to ensure that the choice of options does not necessarily determine the choice of stream in the upper secondary cycle while at the same time allowing pupils to explore their interests and aptitudes in ways that motivate them and enable them to make more informed choices about specialisation when the time comes.

We have not answered one fundamental question: Should pupils be placed in different classes according to their choice of options, or in groups organised by level without necessarily taking options into account, or in mixed classes sharing a common core curriculum? We feel that it is acceptable for autonomous schools to be able to place pupils in classes according to their tastes or aptitudes. In all events, there are bound to be some schools where the level is higher than in others. But we do not feel that this organisation should be enshrined in a law which would introduce an excessively rigid and immutable framework. Rather, it is for teachers, as the law on autonomy already provides, to organise classes so as to respond to the diverse interests and abilities of the students.

### Recommendation 3.1

*We urge a flexible approach to differentiation, based on options which do not necessarily prefigure subsequent choices. Early specialisation or streaming should be avoided at all costs.*

*It will therefore be important to avoid using, in the draft framework law, terms for pathways which correspond with those of the different branches of the upper cycle and the implication that the examination on completing the lower secondary cycle might lead to early streaming (at the age of 13 or even 12).*

### Recommendation 3.2

*Assessment may take the form of a state examination certifying that pupils have acquired the minimum competencies set as an objective for all pupils in this educational cycle. There should be no mention of specialisation or of the options chosen during the cycle.*

## Aspects of the reform of school cycles

We have discussed the current system in Chapter 2, noting that too many young people enter working life without a vocational qualification. Another weakness is that regional training becomes all too often a safety net. We believe that regional training should function not merely as a parallel system but as a complement to the school system. That is the direction in which things are currently moving, and the model that emerges from the government proposals, and we can but approve. On these two points we believe that the new system, based on integration and taking account of the rapid rise in the number of pupils entering the upper secondary cycle, should represent a significant improvement and help reduce the number of pupils leaving the system without qualifications to a minimum. This is one of the two major priorities we identified.

The quality of teaching, in view of a further rise in pupil numbers is another matter of concern. The reforms are set to introduce a number of changes. We have already advised against too early streaming in the lower secondary cycle, preferring a more flexible system with options leading to better choice in the upper secondary cycle. Despite the planned change of name, there may well be a loss of differentiation. Already 96 per cent of all candidates, and 98 per cent of candidates from within the system, pass the *maturità*. The risk is that the system will become a five- or six-lane highway to university based on the six *"indirizzi"* – *umanistico, scientifico, tecnico, tecnologico, artistico* and *musicale* – rather than a conscious attempt to assist the transition of all young people from school to work. This is not a criticism of the reforms: simply, we feel bound to draw the Italian authorities' attention to a hazard that other countries have not avoided. But devaluation of a graduation exam differentiated to a greater or lesser extent would be a serious failure for the reform and would run contrary to the initial intention.

We consider first of all that it is essential that technical and vocational paths should preserve their specific spirit and character. Vocational instruction in particular, leading to the *qualifica* from the first year, should remain highly practical and as close as possible to the world of work. We are also concerned at the phasing out of upper secondary teacher training courses (see following section), which currently take in 8 per cent of each generation. What are these young people to be offered instead? We are aware of the existence of experimental courses for trainee teachers and social workers, and such experiments are of interest per se, but we do not feel that they are sufficient to cope with rising pupil numbers. If the quality of classical and scientific lyceums and technical institutes and the special nature of vocational institutes are to be preserved, this segment (and doubtless linguistic lyceums as well) could well become the soft underbelly of the system, accommodating (as in other countries) those who are not accepted elsewhere and who will not be accepted in selective post-secondary education and will hence swell the ranks of university drop-outs. The path should be either given a clearly asserted identity that fits in with the range of existing streams (especially in technical institutes) or else abolished altogether.

One frequently recurring idea in the reform proposals is flexibility and the individualisation of educational pathways. A balance needs to be struck between the inevitable rigidity of a national system which has to provide a clear and transparent framework and the interests, motives, pace of learning and gradual orientation of pupils. We wholeheartedly approve of this intention, and of the emphasis on modules, training credits and the possibilities of crossing over from one stream to another.

However, the documents available to us provide few details as to the nature of the planned measures. Although the introduction of a certain degree of flexibility may be highly positive, it can also present specific challenges, particularly in a system that has previously been so rigid. The meaning of flexibility needs to be more clearly defined. An important purpose of flexibility over time is to reduce the number of pupils repeating years, or dropping out, to a minimum. The introduction of modules shorter than the school year or in specific subjects is welcome. But the ideas of "education debt" and "remedial action" do not seem to have been particularly successful in Italy. Another issue concerns assisting pupils to cross over from one stream to another. In most cases, there are equivalences between disciplines and the barriers are more often formal than real. The first step would be to define possible equivalences, but provision must also be made for "bridging" classes, which we see more in the form of individualised pathways during the school year rather than specific courses dispensed during school holidays, for example (in this latter context, we do not put much faith in "catch-up classes" either). Lastly, there is the more difficult matter of training credits obtained in school, in regional training or in the workplace, a subject to which we will return in Chapter 4. We are very much in favour of a degree of flexibility, but care must be taken to ensure that the vogue for modules and credits does not lead to a loss of quality and relevance, to atomisation rather than flexibility. Objectives need to be more precisely defined and the framework within which flexibility can operate needs to be clearly identified. In fact, all these measures should form part of an orientation strategy which involves the entire teaching staff. It is to be hoped that, beyond the mere dispensing of instruction, autonomy will encourage teachers to participate in team efforts that will make meaningful individualisation and the whole idea of orientation.

### Recommendation 3.3

> We recommend the introduction of a certain degree of flexibility into pupils' educational pathways, so that the education they receive can be adapted to their interests and pace of learning. However, we would emphasise that an accumulation of modules or credits constitutes neither an education nor a vocational qualification.

> We recommend that further consideration be given to this issue so that greater flexibility does not prejudice the quality of education. Broad guidelines should be issued to both schools and teachers.

Another frequently recurring idea in the reform proposals is that of openness to the world of work which, while helping to achieve the broader objective of developing human resources, also helps to prevent schools from becoming isolated enclaves. We are naturally very much in favour of such initiatives. With regard to work experience, which opens the minds of young people to new possibilities, we were struck by the enthusiastic reception given by employers' organisations to the proposal that all young people should be given some form of work experience (Il Sole 24 Ore, 1997). The reaction in other countries would be very different. Clearly, the business sector cannot turn down proposals based on professionalisation and the forging of closer links between schools and business. But we do not see how firms can possibly take in so many young people, most of them without qualifications, and offer them work experience that has any value as training, even of a very general nature. It was hard enough for the vocational institutes or vocational training centres we visited, partly because young people are sent off on work experience more or less at the same time, partly because monitoring such initiatives is expensive and time-consuming for both schools and businesses. It would seem more realistic to focus on pupils in technical and vocational streams or to promote apprenticeships and other forms of classroom/workplace training. In other words, we find the initial intention attractive but the proposals for putting it into practice less so, resembling a preliminary sketch rather than a realistic blueprint for implementation.

## TEACHERS

The quality of education depends on the quality of teachers and the success of reform depends on their support. Consequently, we take a close interest in the situation and prospects of teachers in Italy. In all the different types of school we visited we met competent and creative teachers who demonstrated remarkable commitment, often in difficult circumstances, but also occasionally revealed a certain disillusionment, a certain loss of motivation. It is difficult for foreigners to fully appreciate all the causes, but we believe we managed to identify some of them. In all events, we accord the highest importance to future policy with regard to teachers.

Managing teaching staff is a thorny problem in any country, partly because of the sheer numbers involved, partly because of their educational level, organisation, ability to negotiate with the authorities and political influence. Moreover, teachers represent a significant proportion of the national wage bill, and the number of retired teachers is growing steadily (pension arrangements for teachers in Italy are particularly favourable). All countries encounter problems in managing the number of teachers and steering a course between oversupply and scarcity and nowhere has a satisfactory solution been found to the dual problem of initial and in-service teacher training.

All of these problems exist in Italy, magnified by an excessively bureaucratic staff management system that stifles initiative and dynamism. In some cases, we felt that the causes of disillusionment and disappointment lay in the absence of reform and the lack of prospects for advancement and promotion; some teachers spoke of a "featureless horizon". That is why the reforms currently in the pipeline have aroused so much interest and expectation. We cannot consider here all the issues that interest teachers, but we would like to make a few remarks about teacher training, the situation and status of teachers and some of the opportunities opened up by the reforms.

### Initial teacher training

Until now, secondary school teachers were trained at university, elementary school teachers at *istituti magistrali* (upper secondary cycle level) and pre-school teachers at *scuole magistrali* (the same level). Similar systems existed in most European countries until recently. Nowadays, however, a secondary level education is no longer sufficient for pre-school teachers and all countries, in various ways, have deferred this type of training to post-secondary level. The transition has not been entirely trouble-free, since the system for training primary school teachers was a venerable one, with its own ethos and political influence, enjoying a certain measure of protection. Today, primary school teachers are trained either at universities or in specialist institutions. Likewise, training for secondary school teachers can no longer be limited to the mere dispensation of instruction in a particular subject or discipline; it has to include classroom experience and training in teaching methods. Again, most countries have undertaken similar reforms, albeit in a variety of different ways.

Italy has lagged behind in this area. A law passed in 1990 instituted a four-year university course for primary school teachers and it was decided that secondary school teachers should take a two-year specialist course after graduating. At the same time, the existing system of teacher training institutes and colleges (*istituti* and *scuole magistrali*) was due to be phased out. In fact, these decisions were not implemented immediately, suggesting that Italy has encountered the same problems as other OECD countries, perhaps in an even more acute form. We mentioned earlier the difficulty of abolishing a whole stratum of the secondary education system which, accommodating 8 per cent of an age group, provides a path to the *maturità* and hence to tertiary education. Likewise, the difficulty of setting up a new teacher training system does not eliminate the recurring problems of the present system, such as the number of graduates who have already been waiting for years to take part in the traditional competitive recruitment examination, the number of supply teachers (*precari*) wanting a permanent post, the classification of candidates according to results in the competitive examination and so on. Despite these problems, the current government has introduced a dual structure for training pre-school and elementary school teachers (DPR 471, 1996). The terms of the transition were defined in an administrative circular of 1997 which stipulates that the new system will come into force in the 1998-99 school year. These decisions will doubtless come up against other difficulties. The universities scheduled to introduce teacher training courses may not be able to do so; the role of existing teacher training faculties (*facoltà di magistero*) is not properly defined; the legal or administrative decisions may not have been accompanied by detailed and prudent plans for implementation. Difficulties arising from the difference in levels of training or experience between teachers formed under the old and new system may be expected to continue for many years. But, however that may be, a start has been made and Italy is taking steps to catch up with other countries in this area.

That is the most important point. Otherwise, it is difficult for us to take any sort of position on a subject as complex and sensitive as this one. We cannot help thinking, however, that the planned system might be somewhat onerous. To clarify, the changeover from an upper secondary level training course to what will in theory be a four-year university degree course represents a quantum leap. Many other countries have been rather less ambitious, envisaging a shorter training course which might correspond in Italy to the *diploma universitario* or diplomas from specialist training institutes. Likewise, the two-year specialisation for future secondary school teachers in addition to a (theoretical) five-year *laurea* course might also be regarded as somewhat burdensome. Less onerous and more practical measures might have been equally effective. Although young teachers are well versed in their subject matter, they lack practical classroom experience. This suggests a need for teaching experience in schools rather than yet more theoretical training. Young teachers should be given support and guidance, and should be given the opportunity to meet experienced teachers who can serve as mentors and role models. Making this a reality would mean giving experienced "master" teachers a mission to guide and support new teachers. Similarly, for primary school teachers we recommend that they should take a special diploma course at the university level, one which emphasises subject content, the latest work on child development and teaching techniques, and includes practice teaching under the supervision of a "master" teacher. OECD countries have developed different patterns of practice teaching and its place in initial teacher training. Such experience could inform further consideration of these issues in the context of the reform.

### In-service teacher training

When reforms as wide-ranging as those proposed by the Italian government are implemented, a considerable effort must be made to accustom teachers, parents and administrators to the new order. The fact that the government intends to devote some of the funds earmarked for the reforms to in-service training shows the high priority given to this aspect, at least in the planning stage. We have noted the work of the Regional institutes for educational research, experimentation and in-service teacher training (IRRSAE). We believe that with suitable support by expert staff, and after a re-definition of their role in a coherent national framework, they could provide effective independent support and advice to teachers.

Whereas previously teachers had a statutory duty to teach a pre-determined curriculum (largely a "satisfaction of input" requirement), they will now be accountable for what their students learn (a "satisfaction of output" requirement). This change in focus for teachers is one that will not be easily achieved but any impediment to it must be removed if the reforms are to be successful at school level. For example, there is currently an extensive in-service programme for teachers in Italy, much of it focused on improving techniques. Unfortunately, there is no requirement for skills acquired during in-service training to be applied in the classroom and used, for example, to improve pupil learning throughout the school. Indeed some teachers seem to attend in-service training courses mainly in order to obtain a certificate which entitles them to a small salary increase. Again this approach satisfies an input requirement and not necessarily a requirement to improve classroom teaching. If in-service training is to be effective, such policies have to be changed where they exist and this sort of salary increase has to be made contingent on improved results in schools.

There is evidence from other countries that, in terms of significant reform at school level, the most effective in-service training for most teachers is carried out in school, with teachers working together to improve the school in a specific area.

Trying to bring about changes and improvements on too wide a front too quickly is often counter-productive, so planning for change and for implementing reform is an essential prerequisite. Local authorities should assist schools with this task. Some teachers could be selected for training as "change leaders" in schools but the focus must remain on improving standards, a subject to which we will return in the section on the legislative effects of the reform.

As the reforms are introduced, problems will arise at a national, regional and local level that can be dealt with on a broader co-operative basis. For example, one of the effects of national evaluation will be to find areas of weakness, say in a particular area of mathematics, or where a new item, such as computer skills, is being added to the curriculum. Implementing a plan to bring the nation's teachers up to the required skill level will require action across the entire education system.

In the early stages of implementing the reform it will not be easy to find people able to lead the development of relevant in-service programmes. There will be those within the system who rise quickly to the new challenge and they should be sought out as leaders in the change process. It may also be necessary to establish links with other countries where similar reforms have been implemented so as to gain the widest possible input.

### Recommendation 3.4

*We recommend that the government conduct a review of in-service training policies which will make the system more consistent with the aims of the reforms. This should include the possibility of making financial rewards following in-service training conditional on significantly improved results in the teacher's particular school. We further recommend that the establishment of school improvement centres to help schools in a given area prepare more effectively for reform and that the role of the IRRSAE be expanded and redefined to assist in this process.*

### The situation of teachers

We were struck during our visits by the abundance of teachers and the small number of pupils in their care, and hence by working conditions which would be the envy of teachers in many other countries.

Figures in the OECD publication *Education at a Glance* show that, of all the OECD countries, Italy is the one with the highest ratio of employment in primary and secondary education to working population in employment (3.8 per cent compared with an OECD average of 2.9 per cent) (OECD, 1997, Table B7.1). As Italy also has one of the steepest rates of demographic decline (*op. cit.*, Table A1.1), the pupil/teaching staff ratio in the primary sector is one of the lowest, if not actually the lowest, in all the OECD countries (*op. cit.*, Table D6.1). Pupil/teacher ratios in Italy are significantly lower than the OECD average at all levels except university. The number of primary school teachers in Italy is continuing to rise even though school rolls are falling. Although this ratio is not directly related to the number of pupils in a class (which also depends on the level and the organisation of the system), it is not surprising that Italian class sizes are among the smallest in the OECD countries and that there is a statutory maximum limit on the number of pupils in a class.

It also comes as no surprise that more teachers should mean lighter workloads. In terms of teaching hours per year, which is only one of the more easily measurable elements of a teacher's schedule, the workload of Italian teachers is significantly lower than the average: between −9 per cent and −20 per cent depending on levels and sectors, the −20 per cent figure corresponding to the *scuola media*. The abundance of teachers also affects pay, and Italian teachers' salaries are also lower than the OECD average (*op. cit.*, Tables D1.1 a, b, c). But in many cases teachers work mornings only and enjoy long summer holidays. Though lower than in some other countries, teachers' salaries are respectable if working conditions are taken into account. We will not pursue this subject any further, for it would require much more detailed information than can be gleaned from international statistics.

Such statistics do provide instructive information about salary scales and increases. In Italy the main, if not the only, criterion for an increase in salary is seniority. Primary and lower secondary school teachers do not reach the maximum salary level until the age of 40. Of the OECD countries, only Spain and Korea have longer lead times; the average age for all OECD countries is 26; in New Zealand it takes only 8 years for a teacher to reach the maximum salary level, in Norway and Denmark 14 years (*ibidem*). *Education at a Glance* (OECD, 1997) also identifies the criteria for salary increases applied to teachers in the state sector. Although seniority plays a more or less important role in all countries except New Zealand, Italy is one of the few where it is the dominant or sole criterion. Training is "sometimes" taken into consideration, but as we have seen, the most that teachers obtaining an in-service training certificate can hope for is a certain degree of geographical mobility and a few extra points on the salary scale. These statistics highlight Italy's extremely bureaucratic approach to the teaching profession, where competence, initiative and results are ignored, and explain why some teachers talk of a "featureless horizon".

Two areas of government initiative have emerged: reducing the number of teachers, taking into account a possible reversal of the demographic trend, and differentiating their functions. The 1997 government budget (Law 449/1997) provides for a 3 per cent reduction in personnel by 1999, though cutting the number of teachers will be no easy matter. Teachers acquire highly advantageous pension rights at a very early stage in their career,[12] but retirement is not a satisfactory solution since their pensions are also paid by the state. Moreover young graduates, including university graduates (as we saw in Chapter 2), have great difficulty finding work; the job security afforded by government employment still attracts many such people. Thus, young graduates supply teachers and those who have passed the necessary examinations but have not yet been appointed are all striving to obtain permanent posts. We have no information on the age pyramid, since this would require specific research that we are not in a position to undertake, but the problem of teacher numbers looks like being a particularly difficult one to solve. Various steps could be taken to try and bring Italy into line with the OECD average, while hoping in the meantime that the OECD average might also move in the direction of the Italian figures. Italy is one of the countries with the highest proportion of university graduates seeking employment in the public sector. Large numbers are also trying to find work in the "advanced tertiary" sector, but very few in the industrial and manufacturing sector, mostly populated by small and medium-sized businesses. One such step would therefore be to limit access to university – Italy is the country with the highest proportion of young people enrolling in universities – and to expand post-secondary paths leading to careers in sectors other than the public sector. There looks to be little room for manoeuvre in the short to medium term, however, especially in view of prevailing demographic trends.

Of course, encouraging professional competence implies impartial evaluation, a highly sensitive issue. As we shall see in Chapter 5, evaluation is the necessary corollary of autonomy and the purpose of evaluation, as expressed in the first paragraph of the directive of May 1997, is to improve the quality of teaching and the effectiveness of schools. However, many of the teachers we met feared that evaluation was aimed primarily at them, and hence they tended to regard it as a threat. On the contrary, evaluation is intended to identify cases where help and support are necessary and is directed primarily at the school rather than at any teacher in particular. This is the message we would like to emphasise, rather than external evaluation of the competence of individual teachers.

A contractual reform of this nature would be general in scope. But there are other forms of differentiation which, in the context of reform, autonomy and integration, correspond to new and essential roles that the reform proposals refer to as "nuove figure di sistema". We have already mentioned "mentors" or "master teachers" who would be responsible for welcoming, guiding and training young teachers in situ, serving as role models. But there are many others, as we shall see. Within schools, certain teachers will have particular responsibility for careers, for supporting pupils in difficulty, for internal assessment, for day-to-day business that will no longer be handled by the ministry or local inspectorate. At local or regional level, there will be staff responsible for evaluating schools and providing educational support. There will be those who act as an interface between schools and businesses, monitoring pupils on work experience or, more difficult still, setting up structures within companies to accommodate and train apprentices, especially as such structures do not exist in most Italian companies.

We believe that the current management system, while it may have ensured job security and upheld the prestige of the profession (albeit somewhat diminished), has not always provided teachers with a stimulating career environment that encourages initiative and rewards merit. The current reforms represent an opportunity for fundamental change. These changes, which include autonomy, curriculum reform and the reform of school cycles, should be implemented in such a way as to give teachers new horizons and fresh prospects for further development.

## IMPLEMENTING THE REFORMS

Just as we were struck by the quality of the debate on the various aspects of the reform and of the discussions which led to the framing of the reform proposals, so we were baffled by the lack of attention paid to their implementation. We acknowledge that preliminary discussions and consensus on the broad outlines are needed before a reform on this scale can be attempted and that the conditions for putting the reform into practice cannot be considered until such a consensus has been achieved. But a reform is not merely a matter of devising concepts or systems; the most difficult thing is implementing them.

The reforms rightly emphasise the need to strike a balance between urgent measures and a step-by-step approach. But the planned timetable, according to which the reform will be completed in time for the school year 2000-2001 if the laws are passed by both houses of the legislature by the beginning of the school year 1998-99, appears to us to be unrealistic. In our opinion, putting the new system in place will take many years.

Of course, some aspects of the reform can be introduced immediately: the extension of compulsory schooling can be implemented within the framework of existing institutions. Other aspects will take time, but it is possible that time can be saved where discussions have been in progress for a number of years: this could be the case for certain areas of the curriculum, in the primary or upper secondary cycle, for example. But we feel that some very worthwhile ideas are still incomplete and require further development. Examples would include notions such as competency levels (*standard formativi*) and flexibility, which we believe need to be refined.

It is true that a timetable has been proposed but it concerns only the definition of the curriculum for the various years in the educational cycle. In other areas, such as evaluation, changes can only be made step by step, since successive stages of the reform cannot be launched until the previous one has been completed. In view of the scale of the planned reform, it would perhaps be appropriate to find the "critical path" whereby the desired result can be achieved as quickly as possible.

What we believe will take longest are those aspects of the reform which require a change in habits and mentalities, especially, though not exclusively, among teachers. It will take years before changes such as greater autonomy and responsibility, teamwork and teaching methods based not on the transmission but on the acquisition of knowledge can be truly assimilated and put into practice. This implies that priorities will have to be defined and support programmes established.

A fund for the improvement and development of education (Law 440/1997) has recently been created, credited with 100 billion lire in 1997, 400 billion in 1998 and 345 billion from 1999. The purpose of the fund is to facilitate implementation of the reform in all its aspects. Of course, it should be used to fund practical initiatives on the ground, but we suggest that it should also be used to fund strategic planning and a detailed analysis of the conditions for implementing the reform.

*Annex*

# APPROVED REFORMS AND REFORM PROPOSALS

Reform of the examinations at the end of upper secondary education (*riforma degli esami di* Maturità)

– Act No. 425, 10/12/1997

Reform of initial teacher training (primary education)

– Act No. 341, 19/11/1990, Art. 3: definition of the university course for primary and pre-primary school teacher-training

– Decree No. 471, 31/7/1996: curriculum of the above university decree

– Decree 10/3/1997: starting from 1998/99. *Istituti and Scuole Magistrali* will be no more responsible for initial teacher training

Reform of the education system (*riforma dei cicli*)

– Bill (*Atto della Camera*) No. 3952, 4/7/1997

Reform of the "teaching content" (*Riforma dei "Saperi"*)

– Ministerial Decree No. 50, 21/1/1997 and No. 84, 5/2/1997 (*Commissione dei Saggi*)

National Service for Quality in Education

– Ministerial "*Direttiva*" No. 307, 31/5/1997

# 4

# THE TRANSITION TO WORK

## DEVELOPING SKILLS

For any country, the development of the skills of its people is a high priority. Improved levels of skills in the workplace improve productivity and competitiveness. Improved skills for living enhance people's quality of life and in the end make them less dependent on government support. It is clear that in Italy there is a desire to achieve a sensible integration of skills for work and skills for life through the provision of effective teaching and learning at all levels in the country. Although there is still considerable emphasis on "front end learning", that is, learning before the transition to work, the needs for lifelong learning are becoming increasingly accepted. In this context, Italy is giving high priority to the ongoing development of the skill level of its people. This focus, which has been endorsed by the other political parties, is backed by business and industry. Such cross sectoral support will be essential if the aims of the government are to be implemented smoothly.

Three reasons for this consensus were given in Chapter 2, a desire to overcome as far as possible any lag in the average level of education in Italy's adult population; the need to extend coverage of the school system and the regional vocational training system to ensure that young people start working life with adequate qualifications; and the need to adjust the structures and nature of technical and vocational education to meet new patterns of social demand and the changing requirements of business and industry. The Italian reform proposals, including extending the period of compulsory education, reforming the education cycles, achieving a more integrated system and the idea of a "right" to education until the age of 18, provide a coherent framework for discussion and action.

In this chapter, we have been guided by the debates that have been occurring in many countries on the most appropriate delivery of vocational and technical education. Their relevance in the Italian context was taken up in Chapter 2. The first concerns extending the period of compulsory education. Attendance in upper secondary schools has grown quickly. This is consistent with trends in most countries. It meets the desire to acquire better general instruction and improve preparation for work. It allows greater emphasis to be paid to the development of life skills and more general education. It also means that formal preparation for work is delayed to a tertiary or post-school stage, with young people, in general, better prepared to enter it. An important consequence is that the rise in the number of young persons attaining their *maturità* will lead to an increase in training requirements at tertiary level. For those who find a place at tertiary level, the trend is a valuable one. On the other hand, this overall shift may leave behind those young people who lack sufficient preparation, motivation or maturity to undertake tertiary education. Also, those whose interests differ from the mainstream may not be sufficiently accounted for. These changed requirements imply two important responses: the first is to establish a "right" to education and training at least to the age of 18 years and the second is to broaden the tertiary provision on offer by developing non-university tertiary education.

Rates of unemployment among Italian youths are high, particularly in some regions and usually those where post-school educational provision is less well developed. About a third of 20- to 24-year-olds are without work, the second highest rate after Spain (OECD, 1997, Table E3.1). Employment in fulfilling work is an issue for all young people. Government attention is often focused on the least privileged or on young people with the lowest level of education, for they are the ones who have the greatest difficulty finding a workplace. However, other groups of young people are now encountering problems in finding work and this general issue gave impetus for OECD's current study of the transition from initial training to work which focuses not only on the lower achievers, but on the whole cohort. The OECD indicators show that, in Italy, the probability of being unemployed and the difficulty in getting work are relatively unaffected by level of education thus revealing a much more deep-seated problem than simply level of skill. Many countries are facing these problems and are exploring different ways of easing the transition from school to work. One general approach is to offer multiple pathways and greater flexibility, both of which are being explored in Italy as part of the reforms.

The imperative for young people to find satisfying work requires us in this report to give close attention to Italy's needs for job preparation and entry into the work force. This chapter will focus on requirements at the second cycle secondary and tertiary levels.

## POST-COMPULSORY VOCATIONAL EDUCATION AND TRAINING

International developments in vocational education and training have very much influenced thinking in Italy and the various reform proposals draw on these developments. The OECD, for its part, has extensively examined vocational education and training (OECD, 1994a to d, 1996, and 1998).

Vocational education and training may be provided in an enterprise setting, in an institutional environment or a mixture of the two. Apprenticeships are a time-honoured mechanism for a balance between "on" and "off the job" training. No one system is seen as superior, although increasingly a programme which provides a mix of school-based and "on the job" training is seen as more effective. Countries like Italy, France and Japan have placed significant emphasis on school-based training. Others, like Germany, Austria, Switzerland and Denmark have placed more emphasis on apprentice type training. Countries with relatively low levels of formal education and training have, of necessity, to rely on non-formalised learning "on the job".

Each country must seek its own path in deciding the relative importance to be given to each form of training. On the job training must continue to occur throughout life, and with the dramatic changes in technology, workplace practice and skills, employers increasingly are taking their responsibilities seriously. On the job training is the form of training used to prepare for specific work in a specific workplace. It can be narrow providing a limited range of skills which are not readily transferable to other jobs in other places. Where this is the only form of learning available to the relatively unskilled, it is particularly limiting.

Apprenticeship, on the other hand, is a very structured form of training, including not only general and theoretical instruction but also pedagogically organised work experience in an enterprise. The general education component may be provided in a school, an outside training centre or in the enterprise itself. It requires close co-operation between employers, schools and training institutions. Where there has been a long tradition of such a relationship, for example in Germany, it works well although some strains are appearing in attempts to extend the system to eastern Germany and to employers who find it difficult to provide sufficient resources.

Apprenticeship schemes wax and wane in their applicability across occupational sectors, but in our view, apprenticeship, and its variants, are an ideal vehicle for transition from school to work. Many countries are endeavouring to update and upgrade their apprenticeship schemes to make them more relevant to the new world of work. Nonetheless, successful apprenticeship schemes require an "enterprise culture" and close co-operation with employers. This is not widespread in many countries and is difficult to establish, requiring a strong social consensus among employers, unions and training institutions.

The third option, training given in a school, provides an effective way of combining general and theoretical instruction with practical work in the laboratory or workshop. While the school can simulate the workplace and replicate many of its features, it is not the same as a workplace. Where high levels of transferable skills are required, such a system works well. Italy provides many good examples of such establishments. Even so, such a system does not mean that young people have to spend all their time in an educational institution, that is, in an environment that is more education-centred than work-centred. Experience in business or industry can be acquired through outside assignments of varying length, integrated to varying degrees into the training programme. The disadvantage of a looser association with business and industry could be an advantage where enterprises, for whatever reason, are unable to provide enough training places. Italy could profit from focusing on its formal system and expand it to increase the association with employers, bearing in mind that each situation is different, requiring a different response. For each occupation and for each region different combinations will be required, all calling for co-operation between schools, business and industry at the local and regional levels.

Vocational and technical education in Italy, as in many other European countries, is essentially school-based, with the "supply" side rather than the "demand" or employer side being the driver of the system. Although it is not part of the school system proper, initial vocational training provided by the regions has so far been of this type, drawing heavily on "occupational profiles" defined by state vocational institutes. In addition, some 400 000 young people have been taken on as "apprentices", although most receive no structured training, except perhaps in a few trades or occupations. Too many receive no training at all, as pointed out in a recent ISFOL report (ISFOL, 1996). Various proposals aim at introducing training (Law 196/1997) for a wider group. At present, however, the "school" model (in its broadest sense, including regional initial training) is the main approach in Italy.

Regional training is currently turning to more flexible approaches, concentrating on skills needed at the local level or on training or further training needs for specific categories. Although basic initial training is still the target of almost a third of students, many other kinds of courses, with emphasis on flexibility and compatibility with the labour market, are becoming popular (ISFOL, 1997a, Table IV.18). This approach is similar to the thinking behind continuous training, most of which also comes under the Labour Ministry and its regional training system. This development is welcome because it helps various categories of young people to enter the work force – from those who have dropped out of compulsory education to others who hold a *maturità* or *laurea*. The coexistence of two (or three) models should prove a useful complement to each other, applying the principle of multiple pathways providing the opportunities for better results.

The concept of "training modules" is one increasingly being applied in other countries and has found some favour in Italy. The application of the concept varies from country to country and Italy will need to decide its own approach. Modules are a vital part of continuing training, where they are used to respond rapidly to changing demands for skills, to technological developments, to the needs of specific sectors, as well as to the practical difficulty of organising longer and more structured courses. They provide flexibility for training the work force by providing for the immediate development of a specific skill or when grouped, acquiring a speciality. No collection of modules, however, can be considered the equivalent of a well-designed course of training leading to a recognised vocational qualification. On the other hand, a tried and tested training course could, under certain conditions and within certain limits, be divided up into modules or useful units. These modules would then be available to be applied more flexibly allowing specific skills to be developed without people having to learn material they already know or material that is not relevant to their workplace.

An OECD study on occupational mobility revealed the high degree of mobility enjoyed by those who had completed apprenticeships in Germany. The status of *Facharbeiter*, and the reputation of the enterprise in which they had acquired this status, were grounds enough for employers to decide whether they were suited for new jobs (often in a different enterprise or speciality); such employers were not concerned with the details of the courses taken or workshop experience. "Holistic" training is sometimes referred to in this respect, the idea being that training is a complex process. Nonetheless, we are in favour both of making greater use of training modules and of making initial training more flexible. There may well be cases where the two concepts overlap, but two different approaches are involved.

Increasingly, the world is becoming dominated by qualifications and certification in an attempt to ensure wider recognition of skills across countries. Appropriate certification and recognition of competencies is a major issue internationally and Italy is endeavouring to address it as part of the reforms. Fundamental to the current approach is that emphasis is placed on the competencies achieved, regardless of the way in which they were acquired. The best option is a certificate or diploma which guarantees that certain stated skills or outcomes have been achieved. Certification systems are being developed, for example in Australia and the United Kingdom, where this approach has been applied and the qualification reached by various roads (see the Australian Qualifications Framework). In Italy, such an approach would mean that the *maturità professionale* could be acquired through training in a vocational institute, by apprenticeship or by continuing training, or by combinations of all three. It is an attractive approach, given the particular virtues and restrictions of each pathway as well as the way they complement each other.

The proposals outlined are being developed in other countries as part of their reforms as part of an active labour market policy. Such a policy is essential if problems of youth unemployment are to be dealt with effectively and a system developed to provide smooth access to the labour market for young people leaving school. It must ensure that they take with them appropriate documentation which is accepted by employers.

## Reform of the post-compulsory level

The proposed reforms, particularly those extending the period of compulsory education and revising the secondary education cycles, will have important consequences for existing institutions. The reforms need to be seen in the light of the "orientation" cycle in secondary education and the "agreement for work". Further, development at the secondary and post-compulsory levels need to be seen in relation to the emerging imperative for a lifelong approach to learning which seeks to foster in young people a motivation for and ability to learn and calls for universal attainment of a full cycle of secondary education and continuous engagement in education and training in adult life.

A keyword of the reform process (in the broadest sense, including for example the *Accordo sul Lavoro*) is integration. Extension of the period of compulsory education, reform of the educational cycles and the prospect of integration provide a useful basis on which to consider the ways the whole landscape might change and what options could be chosen for the future.

### Educational pathways

All countries are seeking ways to diversify the educational pathways open to young people, and to increase the possibilities for movement between them. Attempts to reform pathways – by introducing vocational content into the general education pathway, by reducing the number of entry points or choices within vocational pathways and building teaching around broader combinations of occupations, or by extending the general education content of vocational pathways – are widely evident in OECD countries.

The focus of national policy debate is on how to make vocational education pathways more attractive to young people. The effectiveness of the general education pathway in preparing young people for work generally receives less attention. Yet in some countries around half of all final year secondary students in the general pathway proceed straight to work and not to tertiary study. The labour market relevance of secondary schooling is an issue for all young people – not just for those involved in courses termed vocational education.

The recent experience in most OECD countries is that pathways not linked to future tertiary or higher education study are declining as students seek to keep their options open for as long as possible. Where the choice between the general education pathway and vocational pathways means a choice between obtaining a qualification that leads to work and a qualification that leads to tertiary study, vocational pathways are often less attractive to young people and their families. Where vocational education pathways generate qualifications that can lead to either the labour market or tertiary study, the demand for vocational education can rise. From a lifelong learning perspective, pathways that provide such combinations of qualifications are beneficial. They encourage students to see the worlds of work and study as intertwined, and to integrate their learning. The effective provision of such pathways, though, requires far-reaching changes in curriculum, pedagogy and assessment, and strong partnerships between schools, enterprises and tertiary institutions.

A critical issue is the timing of the point at which choices among pathways are made. Where the choice between the general education pathway and vocational pathways is delayed until late in upper secondary education, as is commonly the case in English-speaking countries, participation in vocational pathways is low, and the problems associated with prolonged general education become more apparent. Two options are available to address this issue. One is to introduce an earlier separation between the general and vocational pathways, to respond to the diversity of talents, develop them to provide clear linkages between the two, and to ensure that both provide qualifications that lead to tertiary study. The other is to introduce more vocational education content into the general education pathway. Where the general education pathway is long and chosen by the majority of students, and has few recognised exit points to the labour market, the introduction of vocational education content can be a strategy for preventing parts of it from becoming a dead end for lower achievers, and for reducing failure at school. If this vocational content is not designed to provide an employment qualification, then it should be considered as a foundation for actual vocational education at tertiary level.

Italy has two parallel and quite similar systems of vocational training. A certain degree of rivalry thus developed between the two ministries and, perhaps, between the "centres" (run by the regions) and the institutes (run by the state). However, regional training remained numerically weak compared with vocational institutes under the Ministry of Education because it is much less widespread than technical education. The vitality and renewed vigour of the regional training system is of relatively recent date. 105 000 students entered into the first year of post-compulsory initial training, as against 126 000 admitted to vocational institutes (1994-95). The total number of students is 151 000 in regional training, as against 512 000 in the vocational institutes (ISTAT, 1996, Table 7.8; ISFOL, 1996, Tables IV.15 and IV.16).

In the case of initial training following compulsory education, the regional training system has often acted as an important safety net for those unhappy with, or dropped out from, the school system. There is a case to expand the regional training system to attract young people who are marginal in the more formal technical system. The proportion of students in each of the systems will vary from region to region, because of the different needs to be met. If regional training was more effectively marketed, it would grow in status and standing and would stand proudly alongside technical education as a viable alternative. As diversity in each of the two systems increases, distinctions between them will become less and less apparent and less and less important. We encourage diversity and multiple pathways to meet specific needs in specific regions. The autonomy being granted to schools should allow this diversity to strengthen. We would want to encourage both systems to undertake highly co-operative relations with industry. How this may occur will vary from occupation to occupation and industry to industry. It is for the schools and employer bodies in the various regions to work out the most effective approach. We want to encourage elements of the present step-by-step approach, which allows young people to find their place in the system, to choose a path better suited to their needs and one that leaves open the possibility of continuing to learn, both at work and in more formal education settings so that they will continue to develop as people, both in a social and work environment. We also support the trend that regional training is extending beyond simply providing initial training. It must be involved in upgrading skills, allowing workers to develop new skills and offering an expanded opportunity for those who currently gain little more than their initial training in a formal way. These changes are the result of an effort towards greater flexibility to meet the changing requirements of business and industry on the local level, and also greater attention being given to a range of pathways for entry into the work force.

For its part, the school system has objectives that go beyond those of meeting the needs of the local labour market. It must provide all young people with a basic general education, equal opportunities, and qualifications recognised at national and international levels. In addition, it teaches more demanding and structured subjects such as mathematics or mastery of languages that are not vocationally specific but enhance the employability of those who take them and their mobility in finding jobs. We noted many examples of school training successfully establishing close ties with local businesses and industry at post-compulsory or post-secondary levels. Such a complementary process between industry and education institutions was sought, for example, in the final *biennio* of vocational training or for specialised *post-diploma* courses for graduates of technical institutes. This should make the regional system of vocational education much more than just a safety net for the drop-outs or rejects of the school system; it should bring a breath of life, energy and realism to every level.

Only brief mention has been made of apprenticeship or learning on the job, particularly where skill requirements are low. For business and industry at the moment apprenticeship provides a means of short-term recruitment. Whenever business and industry find other more profitable avenues, apprenticeship declines, if not, it expands. It is pleasing to note that the Italian authorities have decided to turn apprenticeship into a proper form of training by making it compulsory to include 120 hours of course study a year and to open admission to a wider age group (16- to 24-year-olds). It is acknowledged that the school should play a part in this training, especially in the general education or non-specifically vocational component which is one third of the total. It has also been acknowledged that the Education Ministry should be involved in certifying the acquired skills and knowledge. While these may be first steps, we believe if they are successful, apprenticeships could form a very important role in the school-to-work transition and bring employers and the vocational education system much closer together.

We do not wish to underestimate the difficulties in developing an effective apprenticeship system. Such training does cost employers and small employers, particularly, can find the expectations burdensome. Government encouragement may be needed, but by far the most effective system is one where employers see the real benefits for them and their industry. There is always the possibility of employers seeking the least-cost option when training employees. In this context, we would be inclined to distinguish between the various options, some with no more than a "light" training component. In our view, the word "apprenticeship" should be applied only where there is significant "on and off the job" training, so that, in time, it would come to be regarded in whole or in part as a means of access to recognised high level qualifications and ongoing employment in a skilled area of work. At present, apprenticeship in Italy still appears to be a sort of active labour force measure rather than a valid means of education and training being undertaken within a work environment. No doubt, other types of training will continue, but we would be inclined to make apprenticeship a new means of training for young people.

Germany with its "dual" system is one with a highly developed apprenticeship system which other countries including Italy have considered emulating. Yet it must be recognised that it is not easy to transfer a specific model from one country to another. Even within Germany, there have been problems in attempting to transfer the experience of the *Berufsakademien* from one *Land* to another. A precondition for developing apprenticeship training is the existence of the relevant "enterprise culture". By and large, we do not think that this is the case in Italy, and employers have remained discreetly silent on the issue. Parliament can decide on autonomy for school institutions, it can set up a framework within which apprenticeships could flourish, but it is unlikely to be able to "force" employers to adopt this mode. It will be a slow, gradual, planned process if it is to be widely accepted.

We would encourage the Italian government to adopt an ambitious policy in this area showing how an apprenticeship system can, in association with other training programmes, lead to various levels of qualifications ranging from the *qualifica* to the *maturità* and then to state diplomas for highly qualified technicians. We will expand on this idea later. Unfortunately, our view is that very few enterprises, at least in the beginning, will be prepared to be involved in such a venture, and much effort will be needed to convince employers of its advisability.

The best practitioners of any vocation are in the workplace. They provide the models of best practice for the neophyte, and in traditional apprenticeship training, these "masters" have had a key role in training. They can provide the required teaching in an alternative to the traditional apprenticeship system by simulating a workplace in the school environment. Under this second system, the school is responsible for the integration of general education, vocational training and practical experience. This is a traditional approach used in Italy and for good students in the traditional occupations it has been successful.

Apprenticeship is not a completely different road. It includes both in-enterprise work and experience, and more general theoretical instruction, be it given in the enterprise, in an inter-enterprise apprenticeship centre, or in a school environment depending on the country and local conditions. This is a much more flexible approach, suited to a wider range of students and occupations. Such training could be set up at the local level, depending on available training and teachers, as well as on the needs of local industries, but it must relate both to national skill standards and norms for various occupations, and at least if the best interests of the students are to be served, the training should lead to one or other of the various levels of diploma with appropriate quality assurances to meet national standards.

### Recommendation 4.1

We recommend that the Italian authorities develop a variety of flexible forms of school-based training alternating between education and work.

We further recommend the establishment of a formal apprenticeship system in addition to current "training on the job apprenticeships" which provide an appropriate mix of learning work skills on- and off-the-job, as well as providing a significant component of more general education, leading to three levels of qualification: the qualifica, the maturità professionale and the post-secondary technical diploma. In addition, in establishing such an apprenticeship system, we recommend the formation of appropriate structures to strengthen the links between schools, employers and their associations.

### TERTIARY EDUCATION AND TRAINING

A major issue in the transition from school to work is the availability of a wide range of tertiary-level programmes and study options. In our view, the extension and reinforcement of diversification in tertiary education constitute key targets for reform. Other OECD countries have taken steps to provide and maintain diversity in tertiary education offerings; so far, we believe Italy has not given sufficient attention to this area.

### The debate on diversified tertiary education

Recognition of the need for diversified tertiary sector is not new. It is interesting to recall that in the 1960s, a Parliamentary Committee had envisaged the establishment of institutes having equal status to universities; many technical institutes had already established two to three year tertiary-level programmes to train "superperiti". The social and economic arguments for diversification, if anything, now go beyond those advanced at the time. The evolving needs of the labour market call for a more diverse profile of tertiary-level qualifications. At the same time, the growth in participation implies a much wider range of student interests and backgrounds which need to be addressed through a more diverse range of contexts, contents and methods of teaching and learning. The expansion of traditional university study programmes, following conventional conceptions, organisation and delivery, serves neither the wider range of student interests nor the needs of the economy and society well.

A word on terminology is appropriate. By "tertiary education", we mean a level of broadly defined studies, usually requiring the completion of secondary education and provided through established forms of higher education but also in other ways through new kinds of institutions, by enterprises and in other non-formal settings or arrangements. The choice of terms is deliberate. Following the OECD's Education Committee, we go beyond the activities of universities or even "higher education institutions", notwithstanding that it is mainly through institutions that tertiary education is provided. Further, we are concerned here about programmes, teaching and learning and the options for and choices of learners. From this perspective, the conventional long university study programme is but one tertiary-level option. Other options include shorter courses leading to certificates or diplomas which may involve closer direct links with the world of work.

The terminology and perspective are important because they help to situate the structural and policy approaches taken in different countries to foster diversification in tertiary education. The range of experience and approach is varied: vocationally-oriented programmes offered in a distinct sub-system of institutions in France, Finland, Germany, Austria, Switzerland, Japan, New Zealand and to a lesser extent the United States, and in development in the Czech Republic; "professional" programmes or institutions which "elevated" from secondary to tertiary education, as in the training of teachers and nurses in Italy, among other countries; integrating within conventional university study programmes vocationally oriented modules or work experience, as in France and the United Kingdom; introducing short university study programmes, such as the bachelor's degree in Denmark; allowing for distinctive programmes within a parallel private sector, as in Japan, the United States, France and Portugal; and the development of more distinctive institutional (and programme) profiles within a single system, as in Sweden, Australia, the United Kingdom and generally the United States. In the latter countries, a significant volume of tertiary-level studies takes place in institutions and settings which exist outside of the formal tertiary education sector (*e.g.* TAFE institutes in Australia, further education colleges in the United Kingdom), and these programmes tend to be vocationally oriented. The point is that countries have taken different approaches – often a combination of approaches – to foster and maintain diversity in tertiary education offerings. The questions to be raised are: Is there sufficient diversity in tertiary education provision in Italy? If not, how can it best be extended and strengthened?

While we have argued that there is a strong case for increasing diversification of tertiary education in Italy, the particular approaches which could be followed are best considered in the light of the national context. There is considerable experience with distinct tertiary-level institutions – a system of non-university, tertiary education – and we believe there is merit in exploring how to foster the evolution of what is presently on offer into a strengthened system. As noted, the features of tertiary education provision which seem most important to develop further are practical and vocational orientations, usually combined with work-based experience; programmes of short duration, including an organisation of studies which truly accommodates part-time study; and more varied teaching methods which emphasise small groups, frequent teacher-student contact and ongoing assessments. While it is not possible to reach definitive conclusions with regard to overall effectiveness and efficiency, the experience in many countries is that students following such study programmes usually complete them and have easier access to jobs. At a minimum, these programmes could respond to potential students who presently face a limited or uneven range of study options.

Non-university tertiary education programmes and institutions do not exist in isolation. As economies in the OECD area continue to undergo structural changes (among which, a relative shift of economic activity – and employment – from public sector to private sector, and from manufacturing to services), an evolution in the demand for, and contents of, different types of formal qualification is inevitable. In such an environment new diplomas and new structures may be less readily recognised and valued by potential students and their parents and employers. However, this need not be so, provided that authorities and the tertiary education institutions concerned prepare the way, fostering appropriate partnerships both with employers and with other tertiary education programmes and addressing the interests and backgrounds of those young and old adults which are not as well served by conventional long university programmes and limited alternatives on offer.

**Possible developments in Italy**

Chapter 2 showed that universities in Italy have a virtual monopoly on post-school or tertiary education. Forty-six per cent of every generation follow courses leading to the *laurea*, although only one third manage to complete them. The high drop-out rate is attributed to the lack of alternatives offered to young people on leaving secondary school and concludes that there is a need for a strong post-secondary education sector. There is wide agreement on this point throughout Italy, but the direction in which the reform is heading does not appear to us to be altogether clear. We will therefore attempt to indicate some possible ways forward.

First of all, we will consider the future of the "university diploma", a three-year course of study of a more vocational bent, that universities have been providing since the early 1990s. This was the subject of a seminar held in January 1997 on the basis of an ISFOL study (ISFOL, 1997*b*). However, we have as yet seen no practical proposals in this area in any of the documents available to us, even though the further development of such education is mentioned in the *Accordo sul Lavoro*. The question is clearly posed in the report of the University Ministry/Education Ministry Commission (Luzzato, 1996). In our opinion, the wealth of experience gained could serve as a basis for evaluation and for considering anew which ways to follow.

As we see it, there are risks to providing this form of education within the university framework. For example, when these new courses with their different approaches are provided by the same teachers, in the same establishment, the tuition given to *laurea* students will not differ greatly from that provided to those in the *diploma universitario* course, with the result that the *diploma* course will not have a sufficiently distinctive character of its own. Furthermore, the diploma course is organised in different ways, depending on the discipline or the university involved. Although in the case of engineering, care has been taken to make the two strands of education distinct and to set up two independent courses of study (Delcaro, 1997), in most cases, students in both strands share some classes but not others. It is therefore not surprising that the university diploma is often referred to in Italy as the *laurea breve*. We would also point out that although two streams are better than one, it still provides quite limited choice when one considers the wide range of student ability and employment potential. The approach does show some acknowledgement of the need for flexibility, but probably not enough to meet the broadening employment needs of the next century.

We are also aware that consideration is being given to ways to reduce the length of university studies and that one of the possible options is to view the *diploma universitario* as an initial degree that would give access to a master's course leading to the present *laurea*. The question is, how many students would end their studies at this intermediate diploma level? Those who do not would be better served by a different approach to higher education altogether. It is not our brief to discuss the reform of university education. Even so, we believe this option goes against the initial concept of establishing an alternative programme of tertiary education by introducing a separate, shorter and more employment-oriented education, one having its own identity, similar to that done successfully in other countries. We would also make the point that the generic meaning of the word "university" will decrease in power as more and more universities broaden what they do. An ideal situation will be reached when university and non-university institutions provide a spectrum of courses to suit the wide range of students and future employer expectations.

In our view, the Italian authorities should consider selecting two or three special professional areas for work towards a university diploma, in order to strengthen its specific character, its job-oriented approach, its ties to the corresponding employment market, its supervision and efficiency. We believe engineering would be one such professional area, partly because of the openings available in the economy and partly because engineering diploma studies have already been developed in a parallel and relatively independent course, and thus stand alone, separate from university higher education. Management and business training might provide another area because of their importance to the economy and the wider needs of the European Union.

To produce this kind of education in a university comes hard against university autonomy and decision making processes. How can universities be forced to give such professional training priority? Many countries have side-stepped this issue by having the government provide separate forms of management and funding for the new types of training, including when they are under university administration. Notwithstanding autonomy and decentralisation, however, appropriate instruments will be needed to monitor whether national priorities or strategies for this expansion of non-university, higher education are being met. In this particular case probably both legal instruments, giving a separate existence to higher education diploma courses that are not university type and financial instruments to allocate a larger proportion of resources to funding such courses will be needed. Universities will do what they can to obtain funds, but they must be monitored to ensure that the purposes of the funds are adequately fulfilled.

It is critical that drop-out rates in these non-university, higher education diplomas are monitored. They should be low. Any comparison with the *laurea* drop-out rate is largely irrelevant. The whole purpose of the courses is to provide an effective pathway to work with employer support using teaching techniques and other support to ensure most students satisfactorily complete the course.

A second comment concerns the passage of higher education diploma holders to further university studies. Of course, some students emerging for example from technical and vocational training may wish to continue their studies, and they should be encouraged to do so, such as by admitting them to research laboratories where they will contribute capabilities and a technical sense that others do not have. As we have had reason to say elsewhere, the high drop-out rate in Italy is a cause of considerable concern. This is wasteful of resources both of the individual who fails and the university. We note that the higher education diploma courses now take in almost half the students who were previously enrolled in the *laurea* courses, but they have to start their studies again at the very beginning, losing credits already acquired. Our suggestion is that the Italian authorities should take a look at the A*nnée spéciale* experiment being carried out in France in some university-level technological institutes, under which students who have already followed university level theoretical studies are allowed to obtain a technological diploma in one year only. These students who were unhappy with, or dropped out from, university were very keen to have an intensive course of practical and vocational training during this "special year". We feel the main aim for Italy should be to give the higher education diploma a distinct vocational value and, where possible, to make admission to the *diploma* course open to those dropping out or likely to drop out of the university *laurea* course, after a year or two.

The vocational aspect of the course is largely dependent on establishing co-operation with local business and industry for such purposes as arranging work experience and fostering exchange of views among teachers and the technical and managerial staff of enterprises. The report on the development of the higher education diploma (ISFOL, 1997*b*) and the assessment carried out jointly with the enterprises (Minerva e Vulcano, 1996) show that a great number of consortiums and agreements have already been set up. The MURST-MPI Commission document underscores the success of the programme, and indicates that ties have been established with regional training authorities, which may help improve contacts between universities offering these higher education diplomas and business and industry.

The higher education diploma course is one option to be considered, but it is not the only one. As noted earlier, extension of the period of school education has meant that training for an occupation is increasingly being carried out at tertiary level. Most countries have not merely two, but a variety of training options at this level, some of which require a high degree of scientific knowledge. Others target more technical subjects. The range covered by training courses which lead to middle-level, para-professional qualifications has widened enormously. Lastly, there are shorter and more flexible courses intended to ease entry into the work force or to provide a special skill required to meet the immediate needs of the local market, such as the *post-diploma* courses in regional vocational training.

An obvious weak point in the Italian structures is the almost complete absence of tertiary technical education. The main issue is how best to meet the country's technological needs. For example, the regional training courses, being close to the needs of local employment, are useful and necessary. They have an identity and a purpose of their own. But there are other needs to be met, such as to train professionals who can meet the national and global requirements of international companies.

In our view, many technical institutes have qualified staff, often well equipped workshops, and a certain long-standing reputation. Since they offer resources, consideration should be given to how to make use of them at tertiary level. On the basis of Law 899/1931, a tertiary training course is already being organised for land surveyors and similar initiatives have been taken in agriculture. It is also envisaged to extend the process to accounting and perhaps to the "industrial" branch. Some universities (notably those that have not introduced university diploma courses) that were initially reticent, are now interested in this approach and have begun to co-operate. The momentum is there, but it must be channelled. Provided trade unions and teacher associations focus on the real purpose of broadening the role of technical institutes, that is, meeting the needs of the growing number of secondary graduates who do not have the motivation nor the academic qualifications to take *laurea* or *diploma universitario* courses, yet whose objectives go beyond short-term specialisation or job-entry training, the reforms should be successful. We believe there is a growing number of such potential students.

A major issue facing the Italian government is how to organise and structure the tertiary non-university sector. At present, some elements exist but each is a responsibility of a different ministry thus making co-ordination difficult. The higher education diploma in universities and special purposes schools are under the University Ministry; technical institutes are under the Education Ministry, and post-diploma courses under the Labour and Regions Ministry. Most countries have grappled with these problems: a few going so far as to establish one large ministry encompassing all education, training and employment. As the extent of decentralisation increases the case for new approaches to co-ordination grows.

We would recommend that Italy establishes a system of technical non-university institutions comparable to what exists in many other OECD countries, particularly in Europe, and representing a real "alternative to the universities". First, success of such an initiative at the national or local level will require that recognition be given to the efforts devoted by public authorities, universities and industry to the development of the *diploma universitario* course; it is not intended that these new initiatives should duplicate existing courses. Second, as shown by the experience in many other countries, neither this rather demanding type of course nor the shorter regional vocational course at this level, can suffice to meet current and foreseeable demand for technical preparation from the increasing numbers of secondary graduates as well as industry.

A first step in the direction of establishing the new tertiary system might be to develop and strengthen these two types of programmes within the existing institutional framework. This might involve giving a specific and independent status to the university diploma course within the university, with a view to strengthening its specificity and giving priority to the development of two or three areas, such as engineering and management; and developing within the technical institutes, for example in the industrial field, a new type of flexible organisational framework, closely linked to the local industrial network, including in the framework of an experimental programme developed in consultation with the social partners at national and local levels.

The longer-term objective would be to create a network of technical non-university institutes, when existing courses of both types could be integrated into such institutes, which could be called higher technical institutes, similar to well known institutions to be found in many OECD countries. The original feature of this institution (although there may be similarities with the Community Colleges in the United States or the Further Education Colleges in England) would be to bring together the first two types of courses mentioned above, and then to add to that an element of continuing training, but linked to regional training. The technical institutes, because of their background, their approach and resources, form the natural basis for the proposed higher technical institutes. The challenge would be for both types of courses to develop a completely new spirit. The combination of these two training programmes, some in three or four years (including outside assignments) and some in two years (according to the training programmes and length of outside assignments), would result in a very strong technical and vocational emphasis.

What are the conditions needed for success in both cases? The first is that the training programmes should lead to national qualifications, universally recognised state diplomas that become an ambitious objective for young people and their families, and a reference for enterprises. The second condition is that the training must be flexible enough to respond to the changing needs of the working world. This implies that although the level of diplomas and the general features of training should be defined and recognised on the national level, their specific approaches should be defined "from the bottom up", depending on the needs of business and industry. In light of these needs, a training programme could be drawn up for a few years then replaced by another, while the same experience could be replicated in another city or province.[13] A third condition for success, in our view, is the ability to draw upon a local "consortium". Technical institutes (or the scientific branch of upper secondary schools), universities, regional vocation training, as well as provincial industrial associations and representatives of small-scale production and small enterprises would all be called upon to contribute to this process. By "contribution", we mean that all players would be involved in defining the training programmes, in teaching, in organising assignments and in performing practical tasks. This will require a flexible and adaptable contractual framework to ensure that the goals of this new kind of training are met.

The climate and will for these training programmes and for the *higher technical institutes* to succeed is now apparent, limited at first to the technological field. It is for the government to put in place the necessary enabling laws, market the new approach, make sure they are appropriately funded and offer qualifications of quality that are nationally and internationally recognised.

### Recommendation 4.2

*We recommend the establishment of a non-university tertiary system of education as a matter of priority to allow a broader range of tertiary options to assist transition to work. Initially, this could build on the experience with the* diploma universitario *in such areas as engineering and management, as well as draw upon the capacity of the technical institutes to develop tertiary courses, including in the industrial field. These two components should become part of a system of independent high technical institutes.*

*We further recommend that, in developing the organisational and institutional arrangements, special attention is given to the flexibility of provision, partnership with local enterprises and local needs.*

*Further, these institutes should be promoted so that parents, prospective students, and employers become aware of their relevance and the likelihood of improved success in the labour market. The government should also monitor closely their development to ensure that they retain their fundamental vocational role and avoid drifting towards traditional university characteristics.*

## ASPECTS OF INTEGRATION

As we have already noted, integration is a keyword in the reform process and one we fully endorse. Our concern is in the process of implementing the concept which is often where good ideas falter. It is our view that the whole system of vocational education and training should be part of a national whole in a number of important characteristics.

### Evaluation

The first concerns quality and hence evaluation of the various means of providing technical and vocational training. The proposals for reform provide for setting up a system to evaluate quality of education in as independent a manner as possible. Although to this point the process of evaluation and monitoring has focused mainly on school education, we believe such a system is just as valid for vocational or technical institutes belonging to the school system. Currently, evaluation relates to non-vocational education at all levels of school. Unless a specific system of evaluation is put in place, it will be impossible to judge the quality or relevance of their vocational component. In fact, there is currently no means of assessing the quality of vocational training, be it provided by the private sector, the state or the regions. Such a situation allows for market variance in what is provided, certificates that have little meaning outside the local region and prepares people insufficiently able to transfer their skills from job to job or place to place.

In our view, a system of evaluation and monitoring with appropriate instruments should be established at national level. Its independence and impartiality will have to be safeguarded as carefully as with the national system for quality in education (SNQI) (see Chapter 5), as it will have to assess training programmes from various departments. Ensuring the impartiality and independence of such processes also deserves as much, if not more, attention than is the case for school education. If such a system is introduced, it will provide data to assist institutes and governments to respond to criticism on the various forms of training to be provided within a more integrated system. We know that some vocational and technical institutes are of poor quality, providing courses that are too academic, unsuited to the needs of a modern economy and largely out of touch with the world of work. The aim of the evaluation would be to identify such institutes and help them as far as possible to return to the requisite standards. In this context, national benchmarks should be established to which the institute can aspire with help available to bring about the required improvement.

Another reason for introducing evaluation is to encourage a flexible approach to individual studies, facilitate transfer from one system to another and provide a basis for recognising the skills and training credits gained. It is not easy to assess and compare skills learned, say, in school environment with those learned during work experience. Many countries are currently grappling with these issues and these could be a source of advice. These regional institutions often teach modules which can be given credit to a more formal course. Evaluation would assist in determining how such modules fit a wider picture to ensure the quality of this basic training.

### Recommendation 4.3

We recommend the establishment of a national system to evaluate the quality of technical vocational training, establish appropriate national standards and monitor institutional improvement in terms of these standards. In such a system, the social partners must be represented at local, regional and national levels.

The primary function of this system will be to ensure the quality of training programmes within the school system and the regional training system, in particular with a view to facilitating exchanges and transfers between the two systems in keeping with their integration and flexibility of individual itineraries.

Another function will be to accredit and to approve training programmes created by local initiatives or associations or by business and industry, in connection, for example, with the development of apprenticeship schemes.

### Certification

Another issue to be considered is the need for a national system of vocational qualifications. Here we refer not to training credits or basic skills but to diploma-level qualifications. Reference was made earlier to other countries that are currently implementing such schemes. All OECD countries provide diplomas stemming from the working environment, of which a frequent example is the basic vocational qualification reached through an apprenticeship scheme. Other diplomas come from school-based study, as is often the case with technical diplomas. With the passage of time, basic vocational qualifications have also moved on to become diplomas issued by schools, and diplomas received from schools or universities have come to be recognised in collective agreements. This does not mean that all difficulties have thereby been resolved, particularly with regard to the introduction of a new diploma, as mentioned earlier. However, in Italy the situation appears inflexible and complicated. It is essential that the system of qualifications has national and, if possible, international currency, that standards are assured when a certificate is granted and employers know exactly what the certificate means.

We believe it to be essential, in the context of integration, for this issue to be discussed openly within the Inter-ministerial Committee. We realise that changes in certification arrangements are difficult to implement. For example, professional associations, in Italy as elsewhere, want their members to keep a monopoly over practice of a given trade or profession. We can understand that the engineers' association would not view favourably the development of the *diploma universitario*, even though reliable surveys have shown that holders of this diploma do not generally compete for the same positions (Minerva et Vulcano, 1996). It is surprising to find the public administrations not recognising a diploma established at the same time as the research doctorate (Law 341/1990). It is also surprising that a trade should be allowed to be practised with no more than the *qualifica*, but that those who continue their studies to the level of the *maturità professionale* emerge with no more than a study certificate (*titolo di studio*) that is not recognised by the labour market. Even more surprising is the fact that the regional training authorities can recognise and validate this certificate provided the state vocational institute meets a number of requirements set by those authorities. The final surprise is to find these qualifications recognised at a regional but not national level. Other countries, of course, have "university-specific" diplomas (distinguished from university diplomas recognised by the state), corresponding to a specific training provided by that university. There are also technical diplomas specific to given regions where, for example, the knitwear or plastics industries are concentrated. However, the system of qualifications should be run by the state not the regions. In a number of countries, such as the United Kingdom, this system is the tool by which contributions to the education and vocational training systems brought by various actors in the "training market" can be integrated into a coherent whole. Just as autonomy implies evaluation, integration implies a system of national diplomas.

**Recommendation 4.4**

*We recommend in the context of decentralisation to regions, and the greater integration of the various forms of vocational and technical education, that a national system of qualifications be established. We further recommend that this system be the responsibility of the body established to evaluate vocational and technical education and that the system equates to significant levels of achievement post-school.*

*Further, we recommend that the system be designed so that students can enter each level of qualifications by a variety of paths: school, regional training, apprenticeship, approved private courses or any combination of these that is appropriate.*

## Right to education

The final question to be raised in this chapter concerns the right to education up to the age of 18 which is part of the draft framework-law. We see this as an important "guarantee" for young people to assist their transition from school to work. Those who stay longer in education gain a greater share of the nation's educational resources than those who leave school early. This difference is marked in terms of skills learned and the ability to enter worthwhile work. The working through of the implications of such a "guarantee" are only just beginning, and the matter was brought up in the 1996 ISFOL report. We note that some elements of the right to education up to the age of 18 are already in place: extension of education in upper schools, re-admission to these upper schools and extending entry to the *maturità*.[14] Although these opportunities are available, they have not been sufficiently developed and too many young people enter the labour market with no qualification. This "guarantee" means that all young people should be able to experience the educational resources of twelve years of schooling in some form or another. For many, this will be the traditional school stream. For others, and particularly for those who dropped out prior to completing school, appropriate skill development either on or off the job, the integration of learning and work coupled with the design of more appropriate curriculum should increasingly be made available. We see this "guarantee" as providing important resources to assist the transition from school to work particularly for those who had previously entered the work force with few relevant skills.

We would emphasise one essential aspect, the follow-up and support structures for young people (discussion of such structures adopted in Nordic countries can be found in Hummeluhr, 1997). Unfortunately, the system for monitoring entry into the working world (EVA) has been effectively abandoned. It would provide the government with a strategic tool just as indispensable as the SNQI. In any case, failing systematic monitoring of drop-outs, it would be advisable that those who drop their studies at an early stage (even those holding a *licenza or qualifica*) be actively followed up until the age of 18, and encouraged to continue their education in a vocational training programme, in the framework of an integrated system.    75 |

**Recommendation 4.5**

*We recommend that the Italian authorities explore more fully the commitment to providing a "guarantee" of 18 years of education and training for all those who wish to undertake it and would profit from it. We believe the application of this "guarantee" will require special measures at school and in the workplace so that all young people may obtain a recognised vocational certificate.*

*Further, we recommend setting up individualised follow-up structures by which the right to education will be implemented at the local level and we further recommend that a survey be undertaken on the implications of this "guarantee" of education to 18 years with regard to the organisation and cost of training, the follow-up system, and the guidance services and that a system be established to monitor school leavers and their job placement so that the "guarantee" can be implemented effectively.*

These are some of the issues we consider crucial if the reform process and the move to integrate all the forms of vocational education and training are to succeed. Italy has a strong basis on which to build its reformed system of vocational education and training. Yet clearly, as in most OECD countries, new approaches are required to bring technical and vocational institutes more in tune with the new economic and social needs of society. A crude measure of the success, or otherwise of a system is the number who drop out and the number who find it difficult to find work. We believe some of the measures already outlined in the reforms and with the suggestions put forward in this chapter will produce a system which will enhance Italy's education and training system to the point where it can become a leading country in this field.

# 5

# IMPROVING SCHOOLS:
# AUTONOMY, DECENTRALISATION, EVALUATION

## AUTONOMY AND DECENTRALISATION

Two dominant themes running through the proposed educational reform are decentralisation and school autonomy.

In this chapter, we explore the impact these themes should have on schools and by implication, on student learning in the context of the major educational reforms that are to be put into effect in Italy. In particular, we review how these themes lead to a process of evaluation based on a fundamental need to improve schools. The trend towards decentralisation and school autonomy in a country as large and diverse as Italy is consistent with trends elsewhere and is one we support strongly. Decentralisation empowers people, creates more innovation, and delivers services more attuned to client needs, a rationale which is also applicable to educational services. Moreover, school autonomy is a valuable tool for adapting education to better specific contexts and for meeting the needs and demands of the diverse groups that have a stake in educational outcomes. In Italy, there are also political pressures towards a more federal organisation of the state, an issue considered by the *Bicamerale*, whose in implementation will have a significant effect on the structure and process of education in the country.

Even so, when talking about decentralisation and school autonomy, caution is needed. Sometimes, autonomy is used as a synonym for decentralisation, considering both as the same phenomenon. Yet, both terms refer to two different realities which should be adequately differentiated. Autonomy as a concept is difficult to implement because it has range of meanings and it should always be interpreted in terms of the situation to which it will be applied. Autonomy should act as a principle to guide change in the school environment rather than be an ideal based on independence.

Decentralisation refers to the process of transferring the responsibility for making decisions from the national to the regional, provincial or municipal level, which also implies managing the financial resources for doing so. The current processes of decentralisation observed in several OECD countries are related to the recent changes produced in the structure of the state, with in some cases the development of a federal (or quasi-federal) organisation. The impetus for starting such a process is usually political and connected with the way in which a country conceives its own national/regional reality and the relations and tensions existing between these two poles. This process is not always guided by, nor takes into consideration, concern with school improvement.

Autonomy on the other hand is the principle guiding the process by which schools gain more responsibility for defining their own goals and/or curriculum and for implementing them. It guides the degree of freedom allowed to single schools for designing and developing their own educational activities. It does not imply a lack of general rules or criteria; rather, it allows them to be considered as a framework within which to operate, not a prescriptive regulation. The core of the debate about autonomy and decentralisation, as far as this review is concerned, is a pedagogical one: that is, how can schools be improved so that students learn more effectively. Any connection with the general political situation or developments tends to be of less concern.

In our view, a distinction between autonomy and decentralisation should be clearly made, focusing the reform debate in Italy more on educational issues. Even more important in the implementation of the reforms, autonomy becomes a guiding principle connected with the crucial issue of school improvement. School autonomy cannot be an end in itself; it provides a means to improve education. Schools, given the opportunity to apply the principle of autonomy, will be in a position to organise their activities better and improve their educational processes and outcomes. This is the core of the autonomy issue. Yet autonomy applied too quickly at school level can become dysfunctional and fail to produce the desired gains. A structured approach to developing school autonomy and linking it to effective improvement is essential if the reforms are to be effective.

Autonomy is not a licence for self-determination at the school level; rather, it implies devolved responsibility to meet national, regional and school targets and a parallel accountability to parents, governments and the wider community. The proposed reform in Italy is consistent with this perspective and the attempts in many European and other countries during the past twenty years to reduce central government control of education. Even in the United States, where the organisation of educational delivery is already highly decentralised to 100 000 school districts, educational reforms in the 1980s emphasised school autonomy. This process has been reinforced in the 1990s, when individual school autonomy has been enhanced through some school choice plans and privatisation. The European reforms have focused primarily on decentralising educational decision-making (management) and, to a lesser extent, on educational finance.

The primary intellectual rationale behind such reforms is to give more control over decision-making to schools as a way of increasing innovativeness and responsiveness to pupil needs. With more local management and financial autonomy in schools, parents should increase participation, and school teachers and administrators should have some incentive to improve quality, both by improving teaching and by using resources more efficiently. In its idealised form, the autonomous school is viewed as a small enterprise that delivers high quality education to a group of local parents by a group of autonomous teachers, both with a clear and shared definition of the children's educational needs.

The example most often used in current discussions of educational decentralisation and school autonomy to illustrate this point is private schooling. Private schools, even when subsidised with public funding, can allocate resources and vary their educational delivery with greater freedom than public schools. Hence, it is argued, by allowing public schools the same kind of autonomy as private, these schools will have the incentive and the opportunity to become as attractive and cost-effective as possible, leading to significant improvements in educational delivery. Simply making teachers and school administrators more directly responsible for their pupils' performance and allowing them to implement the changes needed to accomplish this goal, should lead directly to higher quality education.

Yet, despite the widespread belief that decentralised education and school autonomy produce better education, there is no evidence anywhere in the world that such reforms of themselves produce educational improvement. In the United States, where many cases of total public school autonomy continue to this day, studies show no significant effect (Malen *et al.*, 1989). Studies that compare private and public schools with similar social class pupils also show little, if any, difference in effectiveness, unless private schools select their students (for the United States, see Levin and Driver, 1997; for Chile, see Carnoy and McEwan, 1997, and Rounds Parry, 1996).

This should not be surprising. Most public schools world-wide already have significant autonomy in terms of day-to-day-operations, and teachers in classrooms already have a great deal of autonomy and self-direction so long as they cover the prescribed curriculum. Teachers are subject to relatively little supervision in most OECD countries in terms of *how* to deliver the curriculum, as long as they follow the official programme and behave within social norms. Even in Italy's highly centralised educational system, public school teachers and school administrators can innovate if they wish. Some do, with little control from central authorities. Italy's schools are run by adherence to "the law". In such centralised systems these laws are determined centrally and administered at the provincial and school levels. In decentralised systems, with the United States as an extreme, the laws are usually determined at the state or provincial level (for example, California in the United States or Alberta in Canada), and as long as teachers adhere to legal requirements, they can exercise considerable autonomy in the classroom.

Formal accountability in most educational systems is tied to a legal structure rather than to good teaching or good student performance. Under the legal approach it is assumed that if the teacher follows the curriculum and other school legal requirements, the academic result will be acceptable. Unfortunately, a legal system may be exploited by teachers undertaking a legal minimum of work or the legal organisational structure may be more about making things easier for teachers than in ensuring the highest level of educational outcome for students. In such systems, teachers may be tempted to do no more than is required by law rather than do what is necessary to make sure that children learn effectively.

Such an outcome is seen as less likely where schools have the autonomy to allow greater teacher supervision by the community and teacher accountability directly to parents; that is, if parents are prepared to take an active, informed role about what goes on in schools, then parents will be able to judge their school's effectiveness from the level of student learning. Yet, even under the best of conditions, where parents and the community demand higher productivity from the schools and manage to achieve it, autonomy may not necessarily result in more innovation. On the contrary, communities may demand less innovation and stricter adherence to the rules, to traditional teaching methods and to judging educational outcomes in terms of student knowledge of basic skills.

There is a considerable element of this pressure in the Italian reforms. Rather than being based on a strong desire to bring about pedagogical change, many of the reforms of the 1980s and 1990s in OECD countries had strong elements of devolving management and financial responsibility to the provinces and municipalities because central governments expected these sub-jurisdictions to bear a greater share of educational costs and a greater share of the responsibility for the efficient use of resources. This came either as pressure at the centre or from enhanced expectations at the regional or local level. For example, the recent Spanish decentralisation reform was largely a response to certain provinces demanding greater management and financial control over the delivery of social services for cultural as well as economic reasons.

Experience with finance-driven decentralisation without a corresponding focus on improving schools indicates that although financial goals may be achieved, when accompanied by slower growth in funding for schools or reduced financial and technical assistance from the central government to locally run schools, it tends to increase inequality in educational performance between the poorer regions or municipalities and the richer ones (Carnoy and Castro, 1997). Countries that have gone through that experience historically, such as the United States, or more recently, such as the United Kingdom and Chile, are all considering or even enacting *decentralising* educational improvement efforts, suggesting that financially driven decentralisation without sufficient attention being paid to the pedagogical issues associated with it are unlikely to be effective. Italy can gain much in implementing its own reforms from these experiences in other countries, and ensuring a dual focus – on financial decentralisation and on school improvement.

Decentralisation and school autonomy may evoke educational improvement at the local level, but generally only under conditions where educational spending and central (or regional, in those regions that have such expertise) government technical expertise are increased, especially to poor localities and low-income schools that have less of their own financial and technical/human resources to undertake educational improvements. The widely held assumption that more autonomy will spontaneously produce improvement is not borne out in practice. Although in every country and province there exist schools that excel on their own, the more generally successful cases of educational improvement, such as in the United States in the 1980s and Chile in the 1990s, show that educational improvement is the result of systemic efforts that combine educational evaluation, more and better materials, investments in teacher training, more local supervision to assure that teachers actually implement change, increased parent participation and investment in improving school management, and that this effort is led by some central authority (see O'Day and Smith, 1993; Elmore *et al.*, 1998). It is pleasing to note that in Italy, significant additional funds have been allocated to fulfil purposes similar to these. Without this kind of support, cases of school success tend to be isolated, and are the result of a school leader or a group of teachers with a clear vision of educational excellence and the organisational abilities to put the vision into practice. They are not made more general across all schools.

The *purposes* of the decentralisation and autonomy themes in the present Italian reform are different. On one hand, *decentralisation* is a response to political demands by regions for greater *control over resources* spent on social services, such as education, and would require regional authorities to make decisions not made before on aspects of education management.

On the other hand *school autonomy* is a response to a more general perceived need to *improve educational quality*, with the government focusing reform on improving the quality of education. How best to achieve higher quality schooling is the issue and school autonomy is seen as a guiding principle in this quest. If autonomy gives greater decision-making power to school directors and teachers in order to increase how much Italian students learn in school, then it becomes an important part of a school reform package. Even so, defining the reform has "school autonomy" runs a risk. Teacher unions might use the principle of autonomy to limit the evaluation of school performance or to deny effective accountability of teachers and administrators. Even if parents are involved, they are unlikely without external help to have the technical capacity to judge a school's effectiveness and its performance compared with other schools.

Our team is unequivocal in its view that the reform must specify the goals of school improvement, how they will be measured, to whom school directors and teachers will be accountable in their school improvement efforts, and what rewards and action will ensue, should improvement goals be achieved or not achieved.

## THE REFORM

The Italian school system, prior to the current reform proposals, is character-ised by relatively low pupil-teacher ratios, with class sizes in elementary and mid-dle schools varying between 14 and 25 pupils; full-time contracts for teachers that include 24 hours of classroom and in-school staff meeting time at the elementary level and 20 hours at the middle-school level; a Ministry of Education-controlled curriculum; and a centrally-run inspection system (with relatively few inspectors). We saw schools that seemed to be delivering sound education yet there is little doubt from our observations that teaching and learning could be improved; in most schools 70 per cent of teaching-time is devoted to frontal teaching and 30 per cent to testing. There is enormous variation in the quality of education at the elementary and middle school levels, even for pupils of approximately the same socio-economic background. There is no national system of initial and in-service training for teachers, no planned inspection system for teachers, and Italian school directors are not prepared systematically to be good managers pro-ducing high quality education. Unlike most countries, in Italy there is no evalua-tion of individual teachers on their ability to deliver the curriculum adequately, nor is there any evaluation of the effectiveness of directors; the inspectorate as a rule does not monitor the quality of teaching in the schools. There is also no focus in schools on organising for *improving* the quality of education delivered. This lack will make evaluation of the new reforms difficult. Many educational systems face similar problems where the main issue for major educational reform is how to change a static system organised around maintaining existing traditions and pro-tecting the interests of entrenched groups into a more dynamic system organised for continuous improvement.

We have carefully read the Bassanini Act, which sets the ground for the devel-opment of educational decentralisation and school autonomy in the years to come. Articles 1 and 21 draw a picture about the main aims and directions which should orient this development. It addresses both issues but in different ways. Article 1 is generic, outlining the general concept of decentralisation, while Article 21 develops quite extensively aspects of school autonomy.

Decentralisation is addressed as a generic principle for the general reorgan-isation of Italian public administration. Its implications for the education system are, in terms of the act, that "all the administrative functions and responsibilities concerning their respective districts at present carried out by any institution or administration of the state whether central or peripheral or through other public authorities or bodies will be transferred to the regions and local authorities" (Art. 1). In other words, the management function of central authorities in the field of education will be transferred to the regional and local levels, an important change which will likely have a great impact.

This approach raises the issue of what will be the role and responsibility of the central authority if management is delegated to regions. Obviously, the centre's role will be much more strategic, and provide national frameworks and standards. The act retains state responsibility for matters such as the structure of the system, curriculum, general organisation of schooling, legal status of the personnel. This approach is similar to that adopted in other countries that have moved in the direction of greater devolution, such as Spain. This combination of a core set of strong responsibilities of the state with a wide transfer of management responsibilities to regions and *enti locali* fits with the demands of greater autonomy at the school level, accepting that a common educational core determined nationally is retained. Nonetheless, if the state does not have instruments and processes to monitor the implementation of such a core in practice, then the law will be no more than rhetoric. To give the law "teeth" and to support its intent will require the establishment of a nation-wide system of evaluation, combined with new mechanisms for school accountability and a strong central inspectorate. We will return to some of these issues later.

School autonomy, on the other hand, is extensively developed in a long article of some twenty paragraphs. The principle of autonomy is clearly stated in the first paragraph in the following terms, that "the responsibilities of the central and peripheral administration of public instruction in the field of management of education services [...] will be progressively transferred to education institutions". This statement is further developed by establishing some general conditions and criteria for transferring responsibilities to the regional level.

Paragraphs 7 to 10 are central to an understanding of the term school autonomy. Two main components can be differentiated under that heading. The first is *autonomia organizzativa* and the second is *autonomia didattica*. Both are very similarly conceived with the former focusing on resources, staff and management and the latter on curriculum development and teaching organisation. In theory, these may be separated as ideas, but in practice one impacts on the other. A significant resource decision must affect the curriculum and the way it is taught and a significant curriculum decision must affect the level and distribution of resources. These issues are addressed in Paragraph 8 and also in Paragraph 9 of the act and these concepts will need further development in the coming regulations (see Table 5.1.).

Paragraph 7 of the act mentions educational standards. This reference has created significant expectations in the education community, as we have seen in many of our interviews, and is an issue which will require further clarification by identifying the limits of school autonomy in relation to standards and help clarify the concept which is a relatively novel one in Italian education.

Table 5.1. **Act on School Autonomy**
(Art. 21, L. 15/3/97, No. 59)

| Areas of legislative action | Consequent regulations | Implementation of autonomy and financial support |
|---|---|---|
| 1. Definition of the dimensions of a school to be granted autonomy | Regulation (in course of definition) | |
| 2. Learning, teaching and organisational autonomy | Regulation (in course of definition) | Act No. 440 – 18/12/97 Establishment of fund for enlarging educational supply and for equity between schools |
| 3. Legal powers of principals | Legislative decree No. 59, 6 March 1998 | Act No. 449 – 29/12/97 – Article 40: – reduction of number of teachers by 3 per cent – this money given to schools – no longer fixed class sizes |
| 4. Reform of school bodies and committees | Legislative decree – external bodies Legislative initiative in process – internal bodies (schools) | Ministerial decree (No. 765) for trialling autonomy (27/11/97) |
| 5. Students | Regulation (in course of definition) | |

Another principle stated in the act is that of financial autonomy which requires schools to be responsible for managing their activities within certain budget limits. Until now, schools had virtually no flexibility in the operation of their budget. Funds could not be transferred from one budget line to another even though it may have been in the interests of the students to do so. Under the new regulation, schools will be able to make their own decisions about how to spend their budget, according to their priorities and needs. The act does not say anything about accountability procedures for schools to monitor their resource responsibilities. This is a crucial point which ought to be clearly developed in the coming regulations.

As mentioned previously in this chapter, the implementation of the principle of autonomy at the school level should be developed in a measured and planned way so that it can be effectively managed at the school level and monitored at the regional level for school effectiveness and the national level for regional effectiveness. We suggest that the Italian authorities do not underestimate the risks associated with the implementation of such a comprehensive set of changes. The heavy tradition of central-ism and "top down" authority to the school level will require significant time for staff to learn how to behave under the new conditions. To have the new system fully in place by the end of the year 2000 is probably an impossible task, notwithstanding the reso-nance of the date signalling the beginning of the new millennium. Nonetheless, much can be achieved by then, provided the steps have been planned, are realistic and there are rewards particularly at the school level when key targets have been reached.

We agree with the main thrust of the act. Yet there are significant issues that need to be addressed. The first is a lack of definition of the respective responsibil-ities of regions, *enti locali* and schools. Both Articles 1 and 21 attribute to all of them the current responsibilities of the state without further details. This issue will be taken up in a later section of this chapter. The respective limits of decentralisation and school autonomy are not clear at least to us and certainly in parts of the educa-tion system where there is considerable uncertainty about what schools will be demanded to do and what will be the role of regions, provinces and municipalities in their daily management. Any lack of clarity about responsibilities can readily become a source of conflict unless regions, provinces and municipalities have the same view of school autonomy that the schools themselves have. Also, if there are major differences in the levels of competence at regional, provincial, municipal and school levels to exercise their new responsibilities, misunderstanding can quickly arise. The coming regulations must clarify responsibilities at the various levels if the risk of conflicting interpretations is to be avoided.

Although many schools currently exhibit greater autonomy than the law allowed, this is a far step from the creation of a culture of autonomy that is consistent with the new act. The principle of autonomy requires a co-operative pro-cess of decision-making, in which all interested audiences, teachers, parents, employers, students are involved, including the development of adequate govern-ing bodies in which representatives of these groups all may participate. Although Paragraph 15 of the act addresses this issue, more explication will be needed if it is to be applied effectively. As in many countries, the tradition of individualism is alive in Italy whether at an individual teacher or school level. The core of autonomy is team work, not individuality, whether it be between teachers, teaching departments or schools. Co-operation and openness are key principles.

To apply these principles, the aims and priorities of the school, its connection with the local community, the application of its resources to the curriculum all must be reflected on within a framework of school improvement. The "school project" approach used in some other countries, such as France or Spain, can focus this reflective activity and provide a useful tool for accountability.

A critical issue we identified is the apparent lack of a more explicit connection between autonomy and improvement. We have noted that giving schools more autonomy does not necessarily result in their improving teaching. We believe for the granting of autonomy to be successful, a clear and strong connection must be made between autonomy and improving schools. Among other things, this requires a stronger emphasis on accountability. Schools need to report their outcomes in different ways to provide a "brake" on any temptation to become independent without providing accountability. Writing and publicising a school project can be one of these accountability instruments; a national system of evaluation, with regional and local participation, strong support services to individual schools, and a clear set of standards to be met, can also play an important role for public accountability.

The Bassanini Act sets out the principle of decentralisation. The next step is to clarify the principle to the point of identifying the respective responsibilities of the state level, the regional level, the provincial level, the municipal level and the school level. As these responsibilities are determined, they will influence what autonomy will mean at school level. A practical way to approach this task is to identify which decisions should or can be made at the school level and which must be retained at the national level to ensure that the needs of the state are met. From these two end points, sensible decisions can be made about responsibilities at the intermediate levels.

This approach is consistent with the pragmatic experimental approach that the Italian authorities seem to have followed. This is our impression after reading the *Protocollo d'intesa* signed by the Ministries of Education and Employment with the regional and provincial authorities of Emilia-Romagna for "the experimentation of a government system at the regional and local levels aiming at co-ordinating the education and vocational training policies". The main characteristic of this accord is to establish a co-ordination mechanism in which national, regional, provincial and local authorities come together to define and solve the problems they will face as responsibilities are transferred.

We consider this initiative as a valuable one in the current stage of designing the process of decentralisation. On the one hand, it does not exclude any of the different social parties interested in education and allows regions, provinces and municipalities to jointly discuss the sharing of responsibilities on education and training for the future. On the other hand, it pays special attention to the connection of this new decentralised mechanism with school autonomy, by exploring different ways in which both can complement each other.

There are two articles of special interest in this *Protocollo*. Article 6 establishes a three-year deadline allowing problems and possibilities of such co-operation to be explored, preventing, we hope, any open-endedness to the reforms and providing a discipline to get the job done. Even if it is not explicitly said in the text, there should be a commitment to producing a set of guidelines based on the experience of this region which can be used to help other regions open a similar process. We believe that such a process is preferable to a "top-down" one. The implementation of such wide ranging changes will inevitably produce conflict which will require considerable good-will among participants to resolve. In our view, whenever possible, democratic deci-sion-making should prevail with the overriding principle in resolving conflict being the best interests of students in schools. We are pleased to note that the *Conferenza Perma-nente* opens the way for people representing groups outside the formal education system to be involved thus reinforcing the intended democratic nature of the process.

The open nature of the process is reinforced in Article 5, which requires the eval-uation of the experience by an independent evaluator. We welcome this approach, because it will mean genuine experimentation, with an assessment of its outcomes, before making further decisions. Nevertheless, we are well aware that there are polit-ical pressures from some regions trying to speed up the decentralisation processes which may well overtake the more measured and open-ended approach envisaged. Also, it should be remembered that Emilia-Romagna is a rich, developed and well-equipped region, and other regions may not have the same capacity to assume a similar approach. Indeed, there is nothing inherent in the concepts of decentralisa-tion and autonomy that mean that they should be applied in a similar way in all regions or in all schools. In fact, the very essence of the terms is the opposite – the process chosen is the one which suits the particular circumstances. Even so, the expe-rience gained will be very useful if properly done, providing guidance but not prescription for other regions.

### Recommendation 5.1

*Autonomy was conferred on Italian schools in the framework of a decentralisation law. Auton-omy, however, is a distinct concept; it should be conceived as one means to improve teaching and therefore implies accountability, evaluation and support.*

### AUTONOMY AND EXPERIMENTATION

In our meetings with teachers and principals, autonomy was supported by almost everybody. We were even told about a survey done in the mid-1990s (by CEDE), in which 95 per cent of teachers interviewed were in favour of strengthening school autonomy. The most widespread feeling and recurrent argument we detected was that Italian schools lack real autonomy because they are proscribed by rigid leg-islation impeding their ability to organise themselves. Some examples were offered, such as the impossibility of schools setting their own priorities when buying educational materials or the requirement to implement highly prescriptive curricula.

Nevertheless, we found several examples of schools acting in an autonomous way consistent with the expectations of the new legislation. For instance, some ele-mentary schools have introduced changes in their timetables by extending to Sat-urdays and/or several afternoons. This decision can be made by the council of the

*Circolo Didattico*, mainly composed of teachers and parents after a process of internal consultation. We also saw groups of Italian teachers organising their own teaching and assessment activities according to the needs of their students provided that there was no contradiction with general regulations. This is consistent with a significant level of professional freedom that has been traditionally assumed by Italian teachers. We do not see it as autonomy in the sense expected in the reforms, nor does it spill over into areas such as financial management and accountability that the new law will require.

During our visit we found experimental curricula or syllabuses being implemented in different schools. In one striking case, at least three different curricula were developed in the same school for different groups of students and, as far as we could detect, without building bridges among them. In some vocational schools we also found some well-established experimental curricula coexisting with traditional ones again without contact among them nor plans to merge the two of them in the near future. Retaining parallel curricula is costly and there must be compelling reasons to do so which should relate to pupil need.

These experimental programmes arose from offers (whether widely publicised or not) made by different branches of the Ministry of Education in an attempt by authorities to overcome the rigidity of Italian education laws and the difficulties for changing them. Once an experimental programme has been offered, schools can apply to be accepted, and then develop it in different situations and contexts. So, for many schools, teachers and principals, the closest thing to autonomy has been until now a question of choice among possibilities offered by the ministry and other educational authorities. It is a first step in the process of developing school autonomy, but quite insufficient in terms of the expectations of the new law.

In our opinion, a major problem with this process of experimentation is that it lacks a clear strategy for change and future development. Such programmes are offered and promoted by different authorities, which introduce them in a number of schools, often without establishing a monitoring system, nor an efficient supervision system, nor a clear plan for the future. Also, participation in some experimental programmes accords certain advantages for schools and teachers, who like to retain their privilege even if the programme had only marginal benefit to students. So, what was conceived as an instrument for change sometimes ends up as being an obstacle to it.

Experimentation can play a key role in promoting innovation across an education system, but it requires following certain rules. First, it is most important to control the conditions and be clear on the outcomes of such experimentation in order to assess possibilities and limits. To launch such a process without setting some control procedures allowing conclusions to be reached after a certain period of time is counter-productive to achieving wider impact from the innovation. These are essential if there is to be any wider impact of the innovation. Second, a plan for integrating the experimental programme into the educational mainstream or discarding it after a rigorous scientific evaluation is critical. If the experimental programme is better than the one it is intended to replace, then plans and processes should be put in place for its wider adoption. If it does not prove its worth, it should be abandoned or replaced.

In our view, in Italy, experimentation has been conceived more as a way for providing flexibility within a rigid system; rather than as a tool for promoting and controlling innovation at school level. The connection between experimentation and innovation has to be clear. This is the line taken by the minister, who has called a halt to the "spontaneous" innovations but has accepted wide experimentation with autonomy, to see how this aspect of the reforms can be put into effect. Autonomy is much more than offering a choice among different existing options; rather, it is a process of developing school self-regulation and improvement in a context of social responsibility and accountability. A system of incentives should be developed for schools showing good practices and developing effective improvement programmes, and perhaps penalties if schools are clearly not as effective as they should be.

Incentives are unnatural in a system that is driven by law; rewards and incentives are an integral part of any application of the principle of autonomy at the school level. This provides a very different approach and one which teachers will need to be educated to understand. Italy's experience with autonomy is closer to *autonomia didattica* than to *organizzativa* which will require changes of a kind that the system has not experienced. To explore the implications of one kind of autonomy on the other is even more difficult but, if satisfactorily achieved, will improve Italy's schools to the point where they will be able to explain to parents and the general public what they have been able to achieve.

**Recommendation 5.2**

> We recommend that for any experimentation in curriculum, approaches to school management and the like, the goals of the experiment must be clearly defined, the results must be rigorously evaluated, and successful new ideas must be disseminated widely for the benefit of the whole system. We recommend also that, when an experiment is to be implemented more widely, a strategy should be prepared, appropriate funds allocated and teachers prepared to introduce the new system.

## DIMENSIONS AND PURPOSES OF AUTONOMY

We pose the question whether autonomy should stretch as far as giving schools the freedom to choose and appoint their own staff. This will clearly not be an early priority in the Italian context, but is one that should be worked towards over-time.

International experience shows this to be a major issue provoking considerable debate in many countries. This issue is even more difficult to address where there has been a strong tradition of central selection and appointment of staff, as in Italy, with teachers being considered as public servants. Cautious steps are required and these will need to involve to the fullest extent the teacher unions. A first step is to give autonomy to appoint the director of a school, as in Spain or in some parts of Australia. Yet autonomy means little until the most fundamental decision of all, the school's ability to choose its own staff, is put in place. If this is not possible in the short to medium term, then it is essential to evaluate the effectiveness of teaching and learning and provide feedback to those responsible for directing the system.

There are fields where autonomy can be more readily introduced and these provide starting points for action. Two examples are curriculum design and development and financial management. Many countries – some of them traditionally centralised, like France and Spain – have established a system in which schools define their own educational goals and instructional objectives and set their own process of curriculum development, through a "school project". This is a tool which gives schools the possibility to adapt the general curriculum framework and teaching activities to their own characteristics and context. The degree of freedom allowed to schools for setting their aims and goals and for translating them into instructional objectives and teaching activities varies from country to country and can also be introduced gradually. Some of this experience has been gained through school experimentation according to the principle of *autonomia didattica* as set by the Bassanini Act.

Another area in which autonomy can be easily and fruitfully introduced relates to financial management at the school level. Even if the greater part of education budget – mostly salaries – is paid directly from the ministry, schools will have some room to decide about their expenses, investments, and other possible sources of income. The experience in formerly highly centralised countries like Spain or France again shows the beneficial aspects of such a measure. One of the underpinning supports for autonomy is that schools know better than central authorities their needs and priorities in terms of resources, didactic materials, accommodation and so on. It is not necessarily a question of giving schools a larger budget: rather, it is giving them the capability to decide how best to allocate their resources to meet student needs. Another initiative could be to give schools the opportunity to decide what to do with savings made in other fields, for instance as the result of a better management of staff. This will have practical application through the decision by the government to cut its teaching force by 3 per cent and allow this money to be used to assist with implementing autonomy. Again, if a school can significantly reduce the number of sick days its teachers take, the saved resource or at least a proportion of it could be fed back to the school. Schools could also use their autonomy to gain some extra resources, whether financial, material, or free labour. Experience has shown there is considerable reluctance in this area until one or two schools take up the challenge and can show the significant advantages that accrue. Autonomy in this field has to be balanced by a proper system of control and financial accountability and by a mechanism of *assegnazione perequativa*, in order to guarantee the right of Italian citizens to equality of opportunities. In the recent legislation, the responsibilities of principals of schools have been set down giving them the power to achieve some of these results.

One concern we have is that school autonomy may introduce new inequities in the education system. At the heart of this fear is the confusion between independence and autonomy and the relation to accountability. Central regulations will still be valid, but they will provide a general framework rather than be a prescriptive directive. Autonomy implies reinforcing links among schools, at a municipal, provincial or regional level. This is a crucial issue not only for schools at the same level, but between schools from different levels in the same region. One frequent complaint during our visit was the lack of good connections between the different types of schools: principals and teachers of elementary schools think that intermediate schools do not value enough the work they do. The same applies to intermediate schools and *licei*. Schools are not islands: they are parts of networks which learn from and support each other.

Autonomy implies reinforcing the participation of different educational actors in the decision-making process. In some cases, we observed that the participation of schools in experimental programmes was decided solely by principals and teachers, and in many cases by a very small group of these, without consultation with parents or student bodies. Parents often resented such a heavy handed approach but were not aware how the situation could be addressed. The development of school autonomy implies strengthening community involvement and particularly parent and student participation in school life and its decision-making processes as well involving all school staff. Such participation will have to be developed over a long period of time. In the short-run the main action will have to come from education authorities; part of what they need to do is to give better and more information to parents.

Giving autonomy to schools for strengthening self-management also implies offering them a good and efficient support system. Schools need some guidance and help to develop an autonomous organisation, especially during the transition period. Inspectors and some other experts working at a regional or provincial level could well be critical players in the change process. It will also be essential to orientate in-service teacher training activities in the direction of developing the skills needed to implement the autonomy principle. A good training and an effective support system for principals is another key aspect for adequately developing school autonomy, particularly in the school management and resource areas. The new system will need highly professional principals. This will require on-going training of this group giving them the concepts, approaches and instruments needed to develop their role in a context of growing school autonomy.

The process of enhancing school autonomy must be closely linked with measures aimed at school improvement. Initiatives to be adopted in this area must be coherent and specific. It is essential that the reforms link school autonomy and educational evaluation directly and clearly to the objectives of *school improvement and school accountability*. The objective of school improvement means that all schools should strive for excellence, and that they should be accountable to pupils, parents, and society for this excellence in a transparent and meaningful way.

School improvement and accountability require four key elements:

– A national evaluation system that indicates how well children in a particular school are learning the required curriculum compared with other children of the same socio-economic background in their region and nationally. Evaluation should be aimed at measuring the effectiveness of schools as organisations, not at measuring the effectiveness of individual teachers. Good teachers can thrive in poor schools and yet make little contribution to the overall improvement of the school. The purpose of the evaluation system should be to help poor performing schools improve and to make sure that schools are *accountable* for pupils' performance. This requires good teachers to operate as part of a team, rather than as successful individuals. Teacher unions, parents associations, and school administrators must be clear that the outcome of the application of the principle of autonomy is a better school. There are precedents for such evaluation. It has begun to be implemented in Bergamo and Trento, for example, with the co-operation and support of the schools and the teacher unions.

– Autonomy for schools (and parent councils in schools) to experiment with programmes that they believe will improve pupil performance.

– Technical assistance provided by the provincial offices of the ministry for less performing schools. Schools that are doing poorly usually do not know how to do better, even when the school director, the parents' council, and the teachers in the school wish to achieve improvement. In a system that regards the official curriculum as its driving technology, little is taught about the more effective delivery of the curriculum, nor about alternative ways of teaching to accommodate different learning styles. Technical assistance should include in-service teacher training and, perhaps more important at first, new kinds of training courses for school directors. Again, such programmes should be linked directly to improving performance by pupils and to specific issues in schools, rather than to raising teacher salaries as is presently the case. There is evidence that the most effective in-service education to meet the criterion of improving a school is that conducted within the school itself.

– Good teachers are basic to the improvement required in schools that we envisage. We also acknowledge that by international standards, Italian teachers are well trained in subject content, but are relatively poorly trained in pedagogy. There are of course many good teachers in Italy but they have developed because of their own efforts rather than through any systematic programme of teaching and in-service. There is an exception for pre-school teachers. Pedagogy in both the *liceo* and the university is taught as a theoretical subject, not in terms of practical application. It is interesting that cooks, waiters, and machine tool operators must do short apprenticeships as part of their technical education, but prospective teachers do not. Better schooling in the longer run depends on better teaching. No new teacher should begin teaching without at least a six-month apprenticeship. There are various ways this can be done, including the concept of "master teacher" acting as mentor or the involvement of the new teacher as part of a teaching team. We encourage experimentation as to the most effective ways of inducting new teachers into the teaching force.

## STANDARDS AND EVALUATION

The Bassanini Act has introduced in the Italian educational debate the issue of standards, a word which is now widely used among educationalists. During our visit we listened to a range of principals, teachers, researchers and experts arguing in favour of setting national standards, considering them to be an important instrument for transparency and school improvement. This is increasingly a trend being favoured on the international scene (OECD, 1995).

The role of national standards is considered to be two-fold. On the one hand, it is a powerful tool for assessing student outcomes in a context of growing school autonomy. National standards allow schools to know the level of achievement of their students at various stages of the educational process. A set of standards also provides an important instrument for the evaluation of the overall education system, as they set national benchmarks which allow comparison. This two-fold view has significant consequences for the implementation of national standards.

In fact, if national standards are mainly considered as an explicit statement of the aims of the education system and consequently an external reference for student assessment, they have to be conceived as objectives expressed in terms of achievement levels (criterion-referenced objectives) and not objectives related to the achievements of students in the same group or school (norm-referenced ones). This means that they have to state clearly the stage of development that students should reach by the end of their schooling in different fields. And this reference to stages of development also implies that they must be stated in terms of skills and capacities to be developed rather than merely as content to be learned. This approach is essential if standards are to become an effective instrument for student assessment and a powerful tool for school improvement.

If national standards are to be considered as a means to evaluate the education system, they must be stated explicitly enough to allow comparisons. The review team does not mean that they have to be stated in specific behavioural terms, nor as a highly concrete statement of attainment targets. They should allow for the development of widely accepted evaluation instruments which implies the establishment of a consensus-building system for setting precise standards and for translating them into evaluation tools.

## THE NATIONAL SYSTEM FOR QUALITY IN EDUCATION

### Background

One of the major aspects of the proposed reform is the institution of a national system for quality in education. We are fully convinced of the need for such a system in Italy, implying as it does that the Italian community wishes to know how effective its education system is and whether its students are reaching acceptable standards irrespective of which school they are attending. Italy, like most countries, could give more focused attention to the quality of education. With the implementation of the principle of autonomy in schools, a system of evaluation which allows quality issues to be addressed in an objective manner becomes indispensable. Proposals along these lines had already been put forward at the national conference on schools in 1990, but efforts at implementation failed to materialise. Clearly, establishing a system of this kind means a change in ways of thinking, in contrast to a system governed by laws, decrees and circulars; a culture of quality in education illuminated by a system of evaluation, like a culture arising from the application of a principle of autonomy, is not acquired overnight. Moreover, there may be a certain degree of reluctance and opposition when such a system of evaluation is put in place, for example from the unions, who may have seen it as intruding upon the professional independence of teachers and perhaps jeopardising their status. We consider objective evaluation as being fundamental to the success of the reform process and welcomes the government's commitment to initiate such a system as part of the reform.

Because of the diverse nature of the country, the different expectations of people in the different regions, and the government's commitment to autonomy and decentralisation, the institution of a national evaluation system is probably more necessary in Italy than it might be elsewhere. Not only should the evaluation system provide the foundation for autonomy, it should be applied to any innovation introduced as part of the reform. For example, the introduction of guidance and counselling, initiating changes in curriculum, or focusing on school improvement all entail significant changes in the way people think and work. New frames of reference and new goals need to be given to teachers, supervisors, and families and students at every level as well. A system of monitoring as part of the process of evaluation is also needed to track the progress of reform, to steer it and to provide support when and where needed.

We are aware of the wide educational disparities that exist in Italy. These are discussed in Chapter 2. It has been argued that with autonomy, these disparities may increase even more. In our view, to provide equal educational opportunity throughout Italy ensuring equivalent educational quality and student outcomes across all schools is a fundamental responsibility of the state. While respecting diversity and local circumstances, the objective should be to ensure that the educational system is coherent, consistent and transparent. Education plays a critical role in cementing national unity and developing national culture. In Italy's case, national unity is a historically recent phenomenon, making national frameworks, standards and norms even more important and they will need hard work and goodwill to achieve.

## Proposals concerning evaluation

The Italian reform proposals for evaluation are essentially contained in two documents. The first is a May 1997 ministerial directive calling for implementation of a system of evaluation focusing in particular on educational quality. An accompanying memorandum stipulates objectives, methods and priorities. The directive underscores how Italy has fallen behind in the area of quality appraisal, and how long it will take to catch up with the other countries. It makes clear that the goal is to improve the quality of education. The other document is a draft framework law for the reform of educational cycles. Article 17 is succinct, stipulating only that the education authorities must continuously monitor educational processes and results against objectives defined at the national level. This is a core rationale for a system of evaluation.

The May directive gives a broad outline of how the evaluation system is to be organised. One important feature is the establishment of a co-ordinating committee, whose members will include directors-general, to be chaired by the minister with the secretariat provided by his private office. This approach reflects the importance attached to the system of evaluation as a strategic instrument of education policy by the government, and emphasises the desire for close links between the implementation of the policy and its evaluation. To achieve this end, the committee makes proposals regarding the objectives of evaluation, specifies the nature of measures to be taken and examines proposals for intervention from the technical and scientific committee. This second committee, set up within the *Centro Europeo dell'Educazione* (CEDE), is made responsible for specifying evaluation methods, monitoring their implementation and reporting on the results. To assist in communication among the two committees, a liaison unit has been set up within the minister's private office.

### Institutional setting

The orientation set by the May 1997 directive reflects a goal to give evaluation a core role in the conduct of education policy. This is shown by the intention to establish the evaluation system firmly within the ministry. The minister chairs the co-ordinating committee; the minister's office is to serve as the secretariat and the co-ordination unit is to be run through the same office.

There are some who may question the closeness of the evaluation system to the minister, who after all is ultimately responsible for what happens in education. Whether this is fair depends very much on the role of the ministry in a decentralised system serving autonomous schools. In a devolved system, day-to-day management and responsibility rests at the appropriate level: regional, provincial, municipal or school. The minister is responsible for allocating resources, developing strategies, planning, setting standards, but not for the management of the system.

This represents a major change from current practice and will require significant education of politicians, parents, teachers and the general community if the changed requirements are to be fully understood. Even so, despite the best intentions of the legislation and its intended implementation, it takes a strong minister to resist being involved in a management problem at any level if it comes to the public eye. One consequence of the process being put forward is for the central bureaucracy and the minister to make sure that problems relating to implementation or management issues relating to schools remain at arms length from the ministry. Of course, the minister may be required to institute an enquiry if a particular issue is of such a nature that a national perspective is involved. Nonetheless, it would need to be made clear that the outcomes of such an inquiry would require action at the level of devolved responsibility, rather than by the central ministry.

For the moment, the arrangements outlined in the directive have no exact counterparts in other European countries, which have taken a variety of approaches towards relations between the authorities and the evaluation system. In some countries, evaluation of education is assigned to agencies which are linked to Parliament or government but are independent in determining their action programmes. This is the case in England, with the Qualifications and Curriculum Authority (QCA, the successor to SCAA) and the Office for Standards in Education (OFSTED), or in Sweden with the Skolverket. Elsewhere evaluation is the job of internal government units, or, to a lesser extent, a corps of professionals who continuously monitor the standard of education and how it functions. There are intermediate models as well, such as Spain's Instituto Nacional de Calidad y Evaluación (INCE), which comes under the Education Ministry but has a board of governors where the representatives of the autonomous communities are in the majority, or Scotland, which has an evaluation committee within SOED (Scottish Office Education Department), on which the various actors in education are represented.

We consider that the minister's hand would be considerably strengthened if the evaluation systems were to be independent. We would therefore recommend that the evaluation system be accorded a more independent status than that now foreseen in the documents we have cited, particularly to ensure a continuous flow of objective evaluation. In this way, the minister and the committees in the proposed evaluation structures will be able to speak freely about education systems or schools that are not performing to an acceptable standard. Their efforts can then be directed at improving the education system and the schools. If improvement is needed, then resources will probably need to be made available. This is a government responsibility.

It was put to us that the Evaluation Committee should report to the Parliament rather than to the minister. While there is some merit in the argument, we do not support it provided that reports of the Evaluation Committee are public and their findings transparent. After all, it is for the minister, not the Parliament to take action and they will be in the strongest position to do so if such reports come direct. To make issues relating to the implementation of a quality education a matter for the Parliament would cause them to become prey to the idiosyncrasies of parliamentary debate about solutions. Obviously the Parliament should be able, if it is so wished, to debate the minister's solutions and their effectiveness. But this would come after the decision has been taken by the person responsible for education on behalf of the whole Italian community.

There would be merit in establishing in Italy a national educational research body that could undertake research projects of a kind where total independence and impartiality are essential. For example, longitudinal studies on what happen to students after leaving school or an independent assessment of various aspects of the school system would give information to assist decision making. Such a centre could be funded from a core grant from government but with the charter to obtain funds from a variety of sources to undertake specific projects.

### Recommendation 5.3

*We recommend the establishment of an independent evaluation system which focuses its activities on determining benchmarks and allowing schools to assess themselves against these benchmarks, developing tests and undertaking testing at the various school stages, and providing advice on where resources should be assigned to achieve more equitable and improved outcomes.*

*We also recommend that the government consider establishing an independent body charged to undertake independent educational research both from government funds and funds from other sources where there is an interest in an independent view of how well the education system is functioning.*

### Implementing evaluation

We are well aware that Italy is only just beginning the process of implementing its reform process and its associated evaluation system. The first issue is to be sure that the particular level to which responsibility is devolved has the resources to undertake the evaluation needed to know whether the education system and the schools are improving in quality and meeting expectations. The provincial level, for example, is in the best position to provide support to schools within its jurisdiction. It also is in the best position objectively to determine which schools need the most help. This does not violate the principle of autonomy in schools: it is an essential support for it so that schools can know quickly those areas where they need to improve and be helped to design strategies to help them bring it about.

The provincial level needs support as well, and this can be provided by organisations such as Istituti Regionali di Ricerca, Sperimentazione e Aggiornamento (IRRSAE) at the regional level, the Biblioteca di Documentazione Pedagogica (BDP) and CEDE with its archives on testing (archivio docimologico) at the national level. These are resource centres rather than active players in the field.

Another aspect relating to the system of evaluation is the heavy emphasis placed in the directive on self-evaluation by schools. We consider this as essential to the improvement of schools, yet at the same time consider that this approach is not sufficient. The risk is that a micro-culture of evaluation will develop in individual schools which then fall back on their own uniqueness, rather than being part of a system of comparison, taking each school's particular circumstances into account. There is no doubt, although the evidence is often subjective, that a school's "users" – students and their families – have fairly good appreciation about its quality; they make comparisons between schools, classes and teachers, and they are well aware of the ones they think are good and which ones are less so. They make these comparisons now on very limited and often biased data. It would be better to be completely open and to set clear rules about how comparisons can be made which are fair to all. We see the inspectorate as having an important role in this regard. If criteria or objectives are proposed, their purpose is not to establish rankings among schools, but to ascertain what could be done to assist schools that are having problems. This emphasis is critical if the reforms are to be successful.

Implementing the new structure resulting from the reforms with its sophisticated system of evaluation immediately poses the problem of having access to the necessary staff and their qualifications. Staff with a whole range of skills will be needed: some will be involved in formulating objectives, developing evaluation methods and conducting surveys. Others will focus on teaching methods and relationships between students and teachers; still others on management and school administration. Public education has a large corps of teachers endowed with talent and devotion, but existing teachers are not necessarily qualified to take on the responsibilities of evaluation. People currently employed in provincial administrations have acquired experience that is more administrative and financial, and they are not necessarily qualified to conduct evaluations relating to school improvement either. There will have to be specially tailored professional training – as the directive mentions, so that there are people available with the necessary skills. One useful approach may be to send people to other countries to gain experience in evaluation techniques. Another would be to bring people in to initiate relevant training programmes.

Another matter we feel warrants consideration is the role of the inspectorate. While the documents refer to it, of course, indicating *inter alia* that the inspectorate should be represented on the co-ordinating committee, and that CEDE could draw on their experience, their role – curiously – is not specified any further. In most countries, the inspector's role was traditionally to evaluate and rate teachers and schools. Today, in Italy, inspectors often perform technical functions in the ministry, in the general directorates, and in the field as well, to assist in their professional development teachers and school directors and to advise on project development or regional or provincial initiatives. Inspectors have, for instance, prepared reports on the experience of various schools with autonomy and on vertical integration models for basic education. It is our view that the inspectorate has a vital, indispensable role to play in the new organisation, but that its missions need redefining to focus their efforts much more on supporting the system of evaluation and being involved in school and teacher evaluation.

### Recommendation 5.4

*We recommend that the government review the role of the inspectorate in the light of the changed expectations of schools relating to the reforms, in particular in supporting the programme for improving schools and evaluating such a programme in terms of outcomes.*

### The tasks for national system for quality in education

From our perspective, we consider that various possibilities should be considered for starting the development of the programme of work of SNQI. We have reviewed this programme and find it too general. Further thinking should be devoted to specify and define the tasks of the system. One possibility could be to implement a nation-wide testing programme to evaluate Italian education at different levels. A random sample of third grade and sixth grade primary students and ninth grade secondary students could be taken to test their knowledge in mathematics and Italian language.

If data were required for direct feedback to all students, and their parents, then the whole cohort at each level should be tested. It is for the Italian authorities to decide the extent of testing they can require. The results of a random sample type of survey would tell the ministry how well Italian students in general, students in various regions, and students of various social class backgrounds, are faring compared to some standards of achievement in each subject set by the ministry. Testing of this kind could also make Italians aware of what their schools, on average, or by region or province, are achieving or not achieving, and in what areas of these subjects students need to improve.

National testing of every third, sixth, and ninth grade class in Italy, and providing average scores by school would perhaps be more consistent with improving school quality from a local perspective. These scores would be "normalised" according to the average socio-economic backgrounds of the students in the tested grade in each school. The scores would be sent to each school, showing how the students in that school fared against other schools in the region with students of similar socio-economic background. This is the testing model used by Chile's Ministry of Education (Cox, 1997). Its fundamental goal in the 1990s has been to identify schools performing more poorly than expected and to assist them in improving their students' achievement.

In the Italian context, provincial education directors should go over the proposed tests with the province's teachers well before the tests are given to students. It would be pointless to apply a test intended to evaluate school performance without the full co-operation of school personnel. We were shown the results of a successful application of a battery of tests in the Bergamo area. These were carried out with teacher co-operation. Average scores were estimated on a regional and municipal level but not for each school, although they could be. Nor were test scores adjusted for pupil socio-economic differences. Again, that adjustment needs to be made in order to give a fair basis for school evaluation.

The results of those tests can help to identify relatively low-scoring and relatively high-scoring schools. The ministry, either through its provincial offices or through the inspectorate or both, can help poorly-performing schools identify the causes of poor performance. If student performance on standardised tests is low, a more in-depth evaluation of school practices in conjunction with school personnel should yield a series of strategies to improve performance. The ministry should be prepared to provide such schools with technical assistance, teacher training, and materials geared to improve practices. It should also consider rewarding schools that improve student performance over time and sanctioning those that do not. Here is where school autonomy can play a crucial role in school improvement. It is equally important to disseminate the successful practices used in schools performing better than expected so that all schools may benefit.

School autonomy in this interpretation means that schools are given the responsibility to improve and are held accountable for the result of their efforts (or lack of effort). Schools can choose their strategies and can choose to ask for technical assistance or not. But ultimately, they are evaluated and held to a standard. Not every choice will be a right one, so the more information that schools get in terms of successful strategies, the more likely that all schools will show gains.

In such a reform, the role of the ministry is focused on providing technical assistance (including personnel training) and implementing the system of rewards and sanctions for improvement or lack of it. It is only if the schools ask for further evaluation and technical assistance would the ministry become involved. But obviously, if the rewards and sanctions are great enough, poorly performing schools would be foolish not to ask for assistance.

**Recommendation 5.5**

*We recommend the establishment of a testing system to assist evaluation with testing to occur at certain key stages or grades and in particular at the end of compulsory schooling. It is for the government to decide the extent of testing: either random samples, or full cohort testing so that each child and his/her parents know the average level of achievement in their school.*

*We also recommend that the results of such testing be made available as school averages to parents and the wider community so that decisions can be taken about how individual schools might be improved, and how best practice from good quality school might be disseminated for the information of a wider group of teachers.*

We stress that we do not wish to see so-called good and bad schools identified in tables. The purpose of the evaluation is to improve schools, not to rank them. Teachers, administrators and parents in a system of school improvement will develop a philosophy of looking at the data before coming to a view on the school. It is therefore essential that the best data are available and transparently so, in order that judgements about the quality of a school may be more readily made.

# 6

# CONCLUSIONS

We had an opportunity to review Italy's education system at a time when the country was engaged in significant reform, not only of education but the whole structure of government. In proposing reforms for the education system, Italy was mindful of developments in other OECD countries. The changing nature of work, the increase in youth unemployment, technological change were all seen as having profound implications for the education system.

Despite Italy's high level of economic development and global competitiveness, there was also a concern that Italy had lagged behind other countries in terms of educational outcomes and that the vocational education system needed reform if there was to be a more effective transition for young people from school to work. This so-called education gap and the need for a more directly relevant vocational education system which more closely involved industry and employers also drove the direction of the reform process.

Few countries have attempted changes so wide ranging and of a kind that would leave no level of education untouched. This has both strengths and weaknesses: strength in that all sections of education will move in the directions proposed by the reforms with the hope that the educational lag will be caught up and even passed. It has a weakness in that to manage change on such a scale could be so demanding that not all the expected changes will be put in place. It is one thing to pass a law, it is quite another to ensure that it is effectively implemented in a country so large, diverse and individualistic as Italy.

Two major principles underpin the reforms: the first is decentralisation to bring flexibility to a rigid system and decision-making closer to where the service is provided. The second is that of school autonomy, where schools become responsible for what they do. Autonomy, too, can be two-edged: it is a positive influence if the autonomy is used to improve school quality and makes transparent what children learn. It is negative if it is interpreted as freedom with no checks on whether the freedom brings improvement.

We have taken the view that decentralisation will improve decision making at the local level and enhance accountability for what occurs in schools at the local and regional levels. Our view of autonomy is that it will become the cornerstone of school improvement; that it will shift the focus of teachers, principals and others involved in education away from laws that define inputs, that is, class size, school organisation, teaching hours, to a focus on benchmarks to decide appropriate learning outcomes for students in schools. Both these principles, if interpreted in this way, will increase flexibility and enhance the opportunity for teachers to teach in ways that best suit the children for whom they are responsible.

Although we gave close attention to the documentation related to the reforms, visited schools and vocational and technical institutions, held discussions with principals, teachers, parents, members of the community including employers and leaders in the education field, we realise that as outsiders we run the risk of seeing things too clearly and oversimplifying, or not clearly enough and so miss solutions that are obvious to those steeped in the Italian system. We welcomed the way everyone was willing to be open in discussion, to show us good things as well as some not so good. Our main regret was that we could not spend more time.

## ASPECTS OF EDUCATION IN ITALY

Italy's education system is centralised, bureaucratic with considerable emphasis placed on educating the best students. While this is an understandable approach in an historical context, the development of a much more competitive global economic environment requires a work force with as high levels of skills as can be achieved for all its members. A core reason for the reforms was to raise the level of skill particularly of young people entering the work force so that they can meet the challenges of ever increasing levels of technology required in almost all employment. Enhancing the level of education for all citizens so that they can more effectively play their part in a democratic society must also be an essential part of the reform.

Italy has raised the school leaving age to 15 years, to be more consistent with other European countries, and has instituted a "right" to education to 18 years for all those who can profit from it. Both these moves, when taken with the decision to begin compulsory schooling in the pre-school one year earlier, to have six years of primary education followed by two cycles of three years of secondary education, indicate that the Italian government is taking seriously the need to provide all young people with valid educational opportunities.

One particularly compelling issue is the level of youth unemployment and the difficulties many young people experience in the transition from school to work. This is an international problem but Italy has a higher level of youth unemployment than all other OECD countries except Spain.

Since many young people tend to prolong their educational careers in order to stay away from the labour market, it is of crucial importance for policy makers to have detailed and continuous information on young people's choices and on

student flows and, in particular, on what happens to those who leave initial education at different stages. The information base for policy decisions and system
monitoring in Italy should be improved.

## REFORMING THE SCHOOL SYSTEM

Another theme underpinning the reforms is lifelong learning. We interpret this
to mean an orientation of curriculum to prepare young people for the reality that
they will need to continue learning throughout their lives if they are to keep up with
the ever changing skill and work demands. We also see a commitment to lifelong
learning as requiring a close focus on student outcomes and what people have
learned recorded in a way that can be brought to the attention of potential employers. In this context, it is suggested that the concept of key competencies be
explored so that all young people achieve a certain level of generalised work skills.

We see the extension of compulsory schooling not so much as a government
requirement that all young people attend school to age 15 years: they almost all do
now. We see it more as symbolic, to guarantee all young people irrespective of cir-
cumstance an appropriate education leading to an acceptable level of knowledge
and skills which will allow them either to move to further study towards their chosen
vocation, or have at least a minimum level of skill that would be required in the
workplace should they leave and to play an active role as citizens in a complex
democratic society.

We would counsel against irrevocable decisions about young people's futures
being made before the end of the lower secondary cycle (end of compulsory
schooling). The curriculum in this cycle should provide options on the basis of
which students can identify their interests and orientations for further learning. In
this perspective, an orientation cycle should not be structured according to hierar-
chical tracks nor should it aim at student selection. On the contrary, before the end
of compulsory schooling young people should be allowed to try out options, to
choose modules from different orientations or to move from one orientation to
another. Schools must be able to assist students in making such exploration and
search processes an enriching educational experience.

### Recommendation 3.1 [15]

*We urge a flexible approach to differentiation, based on options which do not necessarily
prefigure subsequent choices. Early specialisation or streaming should be avoided at all costs.*

*It will therefore be important to avoid using, in the draft framework law, terms for pathways
which correspond with those of the different branches of the upper cycle and the implication*

*that the examination on completing the lower secondary cycle might lead to early streaming (at the age of 13 or even 12).*

We are also keen to see, as part of the reforms, a comprehensive system of assessing students as well as a separate system for evaluating the quality of schools. There are many different ways to organise a school, and in the spirit of autonomy, we believe this is best left to the schools themselves to determine.

### Recommendation 3.2

*Assessment may take the form of a state examination certifying that pupils have acquired the minimum competencies set as an objective for all pupils in this educational cycle. There should be no mention of specialisation or of the options chosen during the cycle.*

We are also concerned that young people who do leave school at 15 years, are unlikely to gain easy access to the work force unless they have had some work experience. We are also proposing greater flexibility in curriculum offerings using vocational modules where appropriate to broaden the range of pathways available from school to work.

### Recommendation 3.3

*We recommend the introduction of a certain degree of flexibility into pupils' educational pathways, so that the education they receive can be adapted to their interests and pace of learning. However, we would emphasise that an accumulation of modules or credits constitutes neither an education nor a vocational qualification.*

*We recommend that further consideration be given to this issue so that greater flexibility does not prejudice the quality of education. Broad guidelines should be issued to both schools and teachers.*

The quality of an education system is dependent on the quality of its teaching and non-teaching staff and the quality of leadership. To put into effect the reforms, teachers are going to have to do things differently; to assess what they do against appropriate benchmarks; to take responsibility in new ways. We place considerable stock on the quality of in-service education to assist teachers and principals come to terms with the reform process.

### Recommendation 3.4

*We recommend that the government conduct a review of in-service training policies which will make the system more consistent with the aims of the reforms. This should include the possibility of making financial rewards following in-service training conditional on significantly improved results in the teacher's particular school. We further recommend that the establishment of school improvement centres to help schools in a given area prepare more effectively for reform and that the role of the IRRSAE be expanded and redefined to assist in this process.*

We are mindful, too, of the tremendous challenge the implementation of the reforms will require. We believe the change process should be planned and implemented in a staged way, and we were pleased to note the special allocation of 845 billion lira over a three-year period to assist in this process. We are also conscious of the need to mobilise support generally for the reforms.

## THE TRANSITION TO WORK

The problems of providing appropriate preparation to assist young people to enter the work force are facing most OECD countries. The Italian government sees the reform of its vocational education and training system as being critical to improvement in this important area. We agree and have reflected at length on issues relating to vocational education. We focus on convergence between types of vocational and technical education with a view to increasing flexibility and the range of opportunities available to young people.

We noted that Italy had only a rudimentary apprenticeship system when compared with those in existence or under development in many other countries. A strong apprenticeship system requires an "enterprise culture" and the closest possible co-operation between formal education and training institutions and enterprises. We believe in the Italian context, such co-operation is not yet sufficient but we consider a modern apprenticeship system so important to assist the transition of young people from school to work that we would encourage the Italian authorities to establish one.

### Recommendation 4.1

*We recommend that the Italian authorities develop a variety of flexible forms of school-based training alternating between education and work.*

*We further recommend the establishment of a formal apprenticeship system in addition to current "training on the job apprenticeships" which provide an appropriate mix of learning work skills on- and off-the-job, as well as providing a significant component of more general education, leading to three levels of qualification: the* qualifica, *the* maturità professionale *and the post-secondary technical diploma. In addition, in establishing such an apprenticeship system, we recommend the formation of appropriate structures to strengthen the links between schools, employers and their associations.*

Unlike many other OECD countries, Italy has placed major emphasis on a university, post-school, higher education system with only a very limited tertiary vocational education and training system. A shift in the university sector to become more vocational, the development of degree granting, non-university, tertiary education institutions, and the opening up of post-school certificate and diploma courses are all ways to improve the skill level of those preparing to enter the work force. We believe that Italy should expand the non-university tertiary sector to meet the skill needs of para-professionals, to provide shorter cycle training more directly relevant to the workplace.

### Recommendation 4.2

*We recommend the establishment of a non-university tertiary system of education as a matter of priority to allow a broader range of tertiary options to assist transition to work. Initially, this could build on the experience with the diploma universitario in such areas as engineering and management, as well as draw upon the capacity of the technical institutes to develop tertiary courses, including in the industrial field. These two components should become part of a system of independent high technical institutes.*

*We further recommend that, in developing the organisational and institutional arrangements, special attention is given to the flexibility of provision, partnership with local enterprises and local needs.*

*Further, these institutes should be promoted so that parents, prospective students, and employers become aware of their relevance and the likelihood of improved success in the labour market. The government should also monitor closely their development to ensure that they retain their fundamental vocational role and avoid drifting towards traditional university characteristics.*

We could not help but note that there were no effective processes for ensuring the equivalence of courses and training from place to place. We believe this to be essential if the government, employers and parents are to have confidence in the quality of training programmes across the country. Benchmarks are needed to compare both within Italy and across Europe.

### Recommendation 4.3

*We recommend the establishment of a national system to evaluate the quality of technical vocational training, establish appropriate national standards and monitor institutional improvement in terms of these standards. In such a system, the social partners must be represented at local, regional and national levels.*

*The primary function of this system will be to ensure the quality of training programmes within the school system and the regional training system, in particular with a view to facilitating exchanges and transfers between the two systems in keeping with their integration and flexibility of individual itineraries.*

*Another function will be to accredit and to approve training programmes created by local initiatives or associations or by business and industry, in connection, for example, with the development of apprenticeship schemes.*

We also believe there should be one national system of certification so that a qualification granted in one place has the same meaning as one elsewhere. The qualification system should be transparent and consistent with similar systems in other European countries.

**Recommendation 4.4**

*We recommend in the context of decentralisation to regions, and the greater integration of the various forms of vocational and technical education, that a national system of qualifications be established. We further recommend that this system be the responsibility of the body established to evaluate vocational and technical education and that the system equates to significant levels of achievement post-school.*

*Further, we recommend that the system be designed so that students can enter each level of qualifications by a variety of paths: school, regional training, apprenticeship, approved private courses or any combination of these that is appropriate.*

We endorse the approach taken by the Italian government to guarantee every young person a "right" to education and training up to the age of 18 years. This "right" should be interpreted flexibly so that young people can choose the pathway that suits them best to achieve a successful transition to work. As part of this process, we believe that the Italian government should track all their young people over the period to 18 years and beyond until they obtain appropriate work.

**Recommendation 4.5**

*We recommend that the Italian authorities explore more fully the commitment to providing a "guarantee" of 18 years of education and training for all those who wish to undertake it and would profit from it. We believe the application of this "guarantee" will require special measures at school and in the workplace so that all young people may obtain a recognised vocational certificate.*

*Further, we recommend setting up individualised follow-up structures by which the right to education will be implemented at the local level and we further recommend that a survey be undertaken on the implications of this "guarantee" of education to 18 years with regard to the organisation and cost of training, the follow-up system, and the guidance services and that a system be established to monitor school-leavers and their job placement so that the "guarantee" can be implemented effectively.*

## IMPROVING SCHOOLS: AUTONOMY, DECENTRALISATION, EVALUATION

We spent some time exploring the implications for schools of the principles of autonomy and decentralisation and the process of evaluation so that the effects of the reforms may be understood.

The critical issue for us was the improvement of schools and we could see that the principles of autonomy could be applied to achieve that end. Essentially, schools have been granted autonomy so that they can improve, not so they can "do their own thing" in an idiosyncratic way. We saw, too, that decentralisation of (say) financial decision-making or management responsibility, without it being tied to pedagogical improvement, could also fail and bring no improvement to schools.

### Recommendation 5.1

*Autonomy was conferred on Italian schools in the framework of a decentralisation law. Autonomy, however, is a distinct concept; it should be conceived as one means to improve teaching and therefore implies accountability, evaluation and support.*

We also saw that there had been a long tradition of experimentation in Italian schools, brought in not so much to improve schools as to provide a mechanism for bypassing the rigidity of the law. We support a strong programme of scientific experimentation and research flowing from the reform process, with the aim to disseminate results more widely to assist school improvement.

### Recommendation 5.2

*We recommend that for any experimentation in curriculum, approaches to school management and the like, the goals of the experiment must be clearly defined, the results must be rigorously evaluated, and successful new ideas must be disseminated widely for the benefit of the whole system. We recommend also that, when an experiment is to be implemented more widely, a strategy should be prepared, appropriate funds allocated and teachers prepared to introduce the new system.*

We support the establishment of an independent national system of evaluation to review the effectiveness of the reforms as they are being implemented. We also see considerable merit in the establishment of an independent research organisation to undertake educational research on longer term questions, such as tracking a particular age cohort from school to work or to carry out projects for other bodies such as employer groups who have an interest in education.

### Recommendation 5.3

*We recommend the establishment of an independent evaluation system which focuses its activities on determining benchmarks and allowing schools to assess themselves against these benchmarks, developing tests and undertaking testing at the various school stages, and providing advice on where resources should be assigned to achieve more equitable and improved outcomes.*

*We also recommend that the government consider establishing an independent body charged to undertake independent educational research both from government funds and funds from other sources where there is an interest in an independent view of how well the education system is functioning.*

We believe strong school systems, and particularly those where a large degree of autonomy is expected of schools, require a strong inspectorate to assist in improving the quality of schools as well as to assess the effectiveness of teachers.

### Recommendation 5.4

*We recommend that the government review the role of the inspectorate in the light of the changed expectations of schools relating to the reforms, in particular in supporting the programme for improving schools and evaluating such a programme in terms of outcomes.*

### Recommendation 5.5

*We recommend the establishment of a testing system to assist evaluation with testing to occur at certain key stages or grades and in particular at the end of compulsory schooling. It is for the government to decide the extent of testing: either random samples, or full cohort testing so that each child and his/her parents know the average level of achievement in their school.*

*We also recommend that the results of such testing be made available as school averages to parents and the wider community so that decisions can be taken about how individual schools might be improved, and how best practice from good quality school might be disseminated for the information of a wider group of teachers.*

We see school improvement and accountability as being fundamental to the reforms, with the autonomy principle guiding the first and decentralisation making the second possible at the various levels of the school system. There are four key elements needed to ensure the success of the reforms in these terms:

– An independent national system of evaluation which allows the level of learning of the required curriculum to be compared from school to school. Such a system will provide the transparency that is essential to the school improvement process.

– School autonomy and self-management which will allow schools to undertake innovative practices to improve student learning and will allow teachers and parents to focus on the outputs of the educational process, rather than high inputs to it.

– Sufficient technical assistance provided by provincial and regional offices to assist poorly performing schools to improve and to disseminate more widely the outcomes of successful innovations.

– Good teachers and principals working as a team are essential if the improvements envisaged are to be achieved. They will need to strengthen their pedagogical skills and develop fully processes and techniques which assist all young people to learn.

We note that the Italian government has voted 845 billion lira over a three-year period as extra resources to assist the reforms and facilitate implementation. We see this fund as ensuring these four key elements are put in place and that the whole change process is effectively planned, implemented and evaluated.

We have also repeatedly referred in this report to the need to mobilise and sustain the support of all the stakeholders – teachers, parents, students, employers, trade unions, the general public, the local and regional authorities, etc. – for the reform process. This will require, on the part of the ministry, the need to implement a substantial strategy to communicate and disseminate the aims and objectives of the strategy. A regular flow of information will be essential if this is to be successful. This is likely to entail some re-organisation within the Ministry of Education involving for example the creation of a highly competent information unit whose tasks will include providing a regular flow of information and explanations to all the stakeholders. In addition, we consider it important that a review of the structure of the ministry should also examine the creation of a professional unit able to provide the data necessary to monitor the reform process.

### Recommendation

*We recommend that the structure of the ministry be reviewed to ensure it is fully equipped to manage these fundamental reforms and in particular in terms of an active communication and dissemination strategy on the reforms and on internal monitoring capability.*

The reform proposals are bold on any measure; they will go a long way towards reducing Italy's educational gap and should provide by early next century an education system as innovative, creative, and successful as the system we see represented in so many of Italy's enterprises. When the education and training system moves forward hand in hand with a country's industries that provide its economic base, there develops a synergy that allows both sides to gain strength from the other to ensure the improvement of both. The social gains and individual opportunities such a co-operative system provides will enable Italy to take its place as one of the highly successful countries in the European Union.

# NOTES

1. The programme was designed to promote literacy in rural areas.

2. This developed into the current science lyceum.

3. Decree 2038/1938, superseded by Law 739/1939.

4. Law 341/1990. The courses were launched in 1992-93.

5. "I 'rubadipendenti' (Quando il dipendente finisce all'asta)" ["The 'staff stealers' (When employees are up for auction)"] in a Vicenza newspaper.

6. Although in one northern province we saw a growing proportion of pupils turning towards industrial technical institutes.

7. See for example the set of articles in the new magazine *Thema* (1997), "Cercasi meccanico, disperatamente" ("Desperately seeking mechanic"). Other articles and magazines focus on other trades and occupations.

8. See in particular *Thema* (1997) or the results of the Excelsior survey of manufacturing industry carried out by the Lombardy industry association.

9. For a list of approved reforms and reform proposals, see the annexe at the end of this chapter.

10. Synthesis of the works of the commission, Roberto Managliano, Rapporteur, May 1997.

11. In Italian the word suggests a subject that is additional to the normal curriculum; to our way of thinking, options generally form part of the curriculum.

12. The government sought to reform the pension system in order to reduce public spending. Faced with the threat, some 60 000 teachers demanded early retirement under the current conditions.

13. In this respect, in the course of another OECD survey, we had the opportunity of visiting Minho University in Portugal. In coordination with industry, this university organises courses that might be termed temporary. A committee draws up the curriculum, contributions to which are requested from relevant departments and enterprises on an ad hoc basis. The curriculum can be modified or cancelled the following year or adapted for users of a different sort. All of these flexible, customised curricula nevertheless lead to the same diploma. The state guarantees the quality of training and the value of the diploma.

14. ISFOL estimates that 13 per cent of young people drop out of school and then come back later to attain the *maturità* (ISFOL, 1997a, Chapter 5).

15. These recommendations figure in the preceding chapters, with the first digit of the recommendation identifying the respective chapter.

# BIBLIOGRAPHY

BARBAGLI, M. (1974), *Disoccupazione intellettuale e sistema scolastico in Italia*, Il Mulino, Bologna.

CARNOY, M. and CASTRO, C. de M. (1997), "Que rumbo debe tomar el mejoramiento de educación en América Latina", *La reforma educativa en América Latina*, Inter-American Development Bank, Washington DC.

CARNOY, M. and McEWAN, P.J. (1997), "Is private education more effective and cost-effective than public? The case of Chile", Stanford University School of Education.

CECCHI, N. (1997), "L'efficacia del sistema scolastico in una prospettiva storica", in N. Rossi (ed.), *L'Istruzione in Italia: Solo un pezzo di carta?*, Il Mulino, Bologna.

CENSIS (1996), *30° Rapporto*, Franco Angeli, Milano.

COMMISSIONE DEI SAGGI (1997), *Le Conoscenze fondamentali per l'apprendimento dei giovani nella scuola italiana nei prossimi decenni, I materiali della Commissione dei Saggi*, Le Monnier, Roma.

CORRIDORE, F. (1974), "L'Istruzione in Italia (dal 1871 in poi)", in M. Barbagli (ed.), *Disoccupazione intelletuale e sistema scolastico in Italia*, Il Mulino, Bologna.

COX, C. (1997), "La reforma de la educación chilena: contexto, contenidos, implementación", Inter-American Dialogue, Programme to Promote Educational Reform in Latin America and the Caribbean (PREAL), Washington DC.

DELCARO, L. (1997), *Diplomi universitari in ingegneria* (CNEL seminar, January).

ELMORE, R. *et al.* (1998), "How schools construct accountability", Consortium for Policy Research in Education, Harvard Graduate School of Education, Cambridge, MA.

FAUROUX COMMISSION (1996), *Pour l'école*, La Documentation française, Paris.

HUMMELUHR, N. (1997), *Youth Guarantee in the Nordic Countries*, OECD, Paris.

*Il Sole 24 Ore* (1997), "Ci vuole un Maastricht dell'Istruzione", 11 October, Italy.

ISFOL (1996), *Rapporto 1996*, Franco Angeli, Milano.

ISFOL (1997a), *Rapporto 1997*, Franco Angeli, Milano.

ISFOL (1997b), *L'avvio del diploma universitario*, Franco Angeli, Milano.

ISTAT (1996), *Annuario statistico italiano 1996*, Italy.

ISTAT (1997), *Rapporto annuale – La situazione del paese nel 1996*, Italy.

LEVIN, H.M. and DRIVER, C. (1997), "Costs of an educational voucher system", *Education Economics*, Vol. 5, No. 3, pp. 265-283.

LUZZATO, G. (1996), "Documento sull'istruzione terziaria breve", MURST-MPI Commission.

MALEN, B., OGAWA, R.T. and KRANTZ, J. (1989), "What do we know about school-based management", School of Education, University of Utah, Salt Lake City, Utah, May.

MICALI, A. (1996), *La selezione scolastica nelle scuole superiori*, ISTAT, Italy.

MINERVA E VULCANO (1996), *I diplomi universitari e le imprese*, SIPI, Roma.

MINISTRY OF EDUCATION (1997), *La scuola statale, sintesi dei dati. Anno scolastico 1996-1997*, Roma.

MOORTGAT, J.L. (1996), *A propos de l'abandon des élèves supérieurs en Europe*, Council of Europe (Paper for the Quality-Equality Conference, Parma, 1996).

MURST (Ministero dell'Università e della Ricerca Scientifica e Tecnologica) (1997), *Sistema statistico nazionale, Immatricolazioni nell'anno accademico 1996-97*, Italy.

OECD (1969), *Reviews of National Policies for Education – Italy*, Paris.

OECD (1983), *Compulsory Schooling in a Changing World*, Paris.

OECD (1985), *Reviews of National Policies for Education – Italy*, Paris.

OECD (1994a), *Vocational Education and Training for Youth: Towards Coherent Policy and Practice*, Paris.

OECD (1994b), *Vocational Training in Germany: Modernisation and Responsiveness*, Paris.

OECD (1994c), *Vocational Training in the Netherlands: Reform and Innovation*, Paris.

OECD (1994d), *Apprenticeship: Which Way Forward?*, Paris.

OECD (1995), *Performance Standards in Education – In Search of Quality*, Paris.

OECD (1996), *Assessing and Certifying Occupational Skills and Competences in Vocational Education and Training*, Paris.

OECD (1997), *Education at a Glance 1997 – OECD Indicators*, Paris.

OECD (1998), *Pathways and Participation in Vocational and Technical Education and Training*, Paris.

O'DAY, J. and SMITH, M. (1993), "Systemic school reform and educational opportunity", in S. Fuhrman (ed.), *Designing Coherent Education Policy: Improving the System*, Jossey Bass, San Francisco.

ROUNDS PARRY, T. (1996), "Will pursuit of higher quality sacrifice equal opportunity in education? An analysis of the education voucher system in Santiago", *Social Science Quarterly*, Vol. 77, No. 4, pp. 821-841.

*Thema* (1997), No. 1, October, Bruno Mondadori, Milano.

VISALBERGHI, A. (1981), "Aspetti generali del sistema scolastico italiano: sua storia e sua organizzazione", *Scuola e Città*, October.

OECD PUBLICATIONS, 2, rue André-Pascal, 75775 PARIS CEDEX 16
PRINTED IN FRANCE
(91 98 06 1 P) ISBN 92-64-16112-0 – No. 50263   1998